# ROSES

Mr Edland, the Secretary of the Association of British Rose Producers, has been growing roses for many years and is familiar with the many problems which arise when one is planning a rose garden or when one intends to exhibit roses.

In his book he deals with all aspects of rose growing, from the preparation of the ground before planting to the selection of the right rose for the purpose. He lucidly describes the all-important operations of pruning and budding, and he has many useful hints to pass on regarding the exhibiting of rose blooms. The list of roses which forms the second part of the book will be particularly useful to those who are bewildered by the great variety of roses offered for sale today.

*An Amateur Gardening Handbook*

## THIS BOOK

### IS NO 6 OF THE AMATEUR GARDENING HANDBOOKS

*others in the series are*

NEW TITLES ARE CONSTANTLY BEING ADDED
EACH 3s. 6d. NET

AMATEUR GARDENING HANDBOOK NO 6

# ROSES

## H. EDLAND

W. H. & L. COLLINGRIDGE LTD

2-10 TAVISTOCK STREET COVENT GARDEN LONDON WC2

FIRST PUBLISHED IN 1953

*The Amateur Gardening Handbooks*
*are published by*
*W. H. & L. Collingridge Limited*
*2-10 Tavistock Street London WC2*
*and printed and bound in England by*
*Hazell Watson & Viney Limited*
*Aylesbury and London*

# CONTENTS

# ILLUSTRATIONS

### BY C. NEWSOME-TAYLOR

# CHAPTER ONE

# PREPARATION OF THE SOIL

MUCH has been written on the adaptability of the rose in varying types of soil; nevertheless, the Queen of Flowers has her likes and dislikes. As can be appreciated, she prefers one of good depth, well-drained and fertile, but as few soils are naturally so, the first necessity is to strive for this happy condition. In mentioning depth of soil, it is not intended to endorse the fallacy that roses can only be grown successfully on a heavy clay soil—this is far from being correct. True, one of clay generally has depth, and it can with extensive cultivation be made excellent for roses, but it is one of the most difficult to work. If the reader ever has the choice, let him select a soil with a loamy top spit containing only about 50 per cent. of clay and, for further preference, with a gravel subsoil, thus eliminating possible trouble with drainage.

These latter remarks, however, are probably for the most part superfluous, other considerations rather than the nature of the soil determining the purchase of a home and garden, most gardeners having to make the best of the plot that falls to their lot. Adverse soil conditions, however, can be improved.

**Digging** The first essential is to get the soil into good heart, and the way to do this is to take off one's coat and dig. Whatever its nature the soil for roses requires to be dug two spits deep and the top soil kept at the top. The lower spit should be well broken up and, if heavy, a generous dressing of hydrated lime worked into it at the rate of 3 lb. to the square yard. Lime may not be needed on light soils, as they are often alkaline, but if there is any doubt as to this, it is easily determined. Take a little of the soil, damp it and then pour over it some hydrochloric acid. If lime is present it will effervesce freely; if there is little or no response, then it requires lime.

The usual way of making a bed after marking it out is to start at one end and take a layer of the top soil, about 18 inches wide and 12 inches deep, and wheel it away and deposit it at the other end of the bed. Then the subsoil thus exposed can be broken up and the top spit from the next 18 inches put on top of it, and so on until the other end of the bed is reached. The top soil deposited there then fills in the final section.

**Supplying Humus to the Soil**   The next job is to work in some humus with the top spit, as whatever the nature of the soil it will benefit physically from the application, and in addition it will provide nutriment for the trees to be planted. Organic manures are best, such as well-decayed farmyard manures or chopped turves, well-decomposed compost, leaf-mould, etc., but if these are in short supply, they can be eked out by mixing them with peat. An alternative is hop manure, which is easily purchasable, and this, too, can be eked out with peat.

The mixing in can be done with the initial digging, but if time permits it is an advantage to apply it with a second digging of the top spit to ensure that the soil gets turned over more than once. There is no doubt that 'cultivation' of this kind is highly beneficial, and as many diggings as possible should be given. Before planting, however, at least a month must elapse to allow for consolidation.

The addition of the organic matter to the beds will raise them above the level of the surrounding paths. In a heavy soil this is an advantage, as it will assist drainage, but with a light soil it would be advisable to remove some of the subsoil first, so that when the bed is completed it is level or even below the surrounding surface. This will assist in conserving moisture.

Possibly the most heart-breaking soil to deal with is one on chalk, and the success to be achieved depends entirely upon the initial preparations and the amount of humus dug into the top spit. Unfortunately, however, humus only has a limited life, and thereafter there develops a continuous struggle against the effects of the excess of lime, which causes a disease known as chlorosis. If the expense can be afforded, more lasting results are obtained by replacing the existing soil with imported soil more congenial to roses. Mix in with this the organic matter to which reference has been made.

# CHAPTER TWO

# PLANNING THE ROSE GARDEN

WHEN planning a new garden do not make the beds so wide that ordinary cultivation cannot be carried out without treading on the soil. The width should not exceed 6 feet, which will permit of three rows of trees, yet be accessible from either side.

**Mixed Beds** Another pitfall is the indiscriminate planting of varieties irrespective of their habit of growth, so that one tree overshadows another. The difficulty can be avoided by planting a separate variety in each bed, thus

1. *A suggested lay-out or centre-piece for a rose garden.*

more easily achieving uniformity, although with care and planning there is no real fault to find with mixed beds. Advocates of the one variety per bed arrangement frequently make a point of the colours clashing in mixed beds, but this kind of observation is more fanciful than true. All, or practically all, colours of roses in their natural environment blend without violating aesthetic tastes. Whereas two colours might clash, the possibility fades with a number of mixed varieties and colours, and the argument against mixed beds can be discounted, provided attention is paid to the individual requirements of the respective varieties.

**The Order of Planting**  It is advisable first to plan the order of planting. It is only common sense if, for example, one is planning for a bed 6 feet wide which will accommodate three rows of trees, to have the tallest growers in the centre row so that they stand out above those in the outer rows. Similarly, it is advisable to stagger the plants so that they are not in straight rows. In Chapter Eleven the very vigorous varieties are indicated, and these should be given a little more space than the average varieties, which should be planted 1 foot 9 inches apart.

**Ramblers**  Do not plant ramblers too closely. A strong plant will easily cover a space 15 feet wide, yet they are often planted as closely as 6 feet apart and in a year or two they are a tangled mass and the despair of the grower.

Ramblers are usually grown on pergolas, along fences or specially prepared trellis-work, but they can be grown in other ways to great advantage. One method is on tripods and another is pegged down in beds. The latter method is seldom used, yet is very effective. Two plants are sufficient for a bed, say 12 feet long and 6 feet wide. They should be planted in the centre of the bed and the long growths trained over to right and left and intertwined. Two varieties such as François Juranville and Léontine Gervais will present a lovely sight when in bloom. For the tripods, larch poles 11 to 12 feet long should be used, and inserted into the soil to a depth of 2 to 3 feet, each 6 feet apart at the base, leaned together and secured at the top with strong wire. Two plants can then be planted opposite to each other inside the poles, and the growths from each trained in the same direction in spiral fashion round the poles. In two or three years the growths will reach the top, after which they can be allowed to fall back or trained along chains from one tripod to another.

Owing to their susceptibility to mildew, ramblers should not be planted against walls, as they prefer free circulation of air through the foliage.

**Climbing Hybrid Teas** The growths of this type of climber must be trained as horizontally as possible to obtain the best results. Grown as pillars, they are inclined to become lanky with what little bloom they produce at a height well out of reach. Furthermore, the lateral growths coming off at a tangent are difficult to tie in, and for this reason are often left; thus they become a nuisance, catching the clothing of passers-by. On pergolas this unsuitability is more marked—the growths on the uprights of the pergolas are more often than not devoid of bloom, and the growths across the top, owing to their inaccessibility, are usually left untended. Thus they point heavenwards with perhaps a few blooms waving about in the air some 10 feet to 12 feet above the ground. For pillars and pergolas use the ramblers, and plant the climbing Hybrid Teas against walls or fences so that their growths can be spread out horizontally. The tension thus created will more readily produce flowering laterals and give greater satisfaction.

**Specimen Plants** Specimen plants grown in their own individual circular plots cut out of the lawn are also most effective, and many of the species are ideal for this purpose, although the blooming period of the species is rather fleeting. They do, however, provide colour in May at a time of the year when there is not a lot to be seen, also the foliage of many is most attractive, and their heps have a distinctive beauty of their own in the autumn. Suitable varieties are listed in Chapter Ten.

**Rose Hedges** Another feature of the rose garden is a hedge of roses in lieu of the ubiquitous evergreen. The Hybrid Musks are particularly suitable for this purpose, as they are perpetual flowering and very fragrant. The *Rosa rugosa* hybrids, too, have similar qualities to the Hybrid Musks and can be recommended. If a more dwarf hedge is required, then we have the Floribundas. Suitable varieties for hedges are listed in Chapter Ten.

Rose-beds are best kept free from other plants, except perhaps for edging plants. There is a great temptation to utilize the rose-beds for bulbs to provide colour in the spring. This can be, and is, done, but the presence of bulbs prevents hoeing and other necessary work.

# CHAPTER THREE

# PLANTING

**The Treatment of Newly Bought Trees**  The importance of unpacking the bundles and getting the trees into the ground without unnecessary delay cannot be too strongly emphasized, more trees being killed through the roots drying out than is generally realized. When the trees fail to respond in the spring, it is usually for this reason. This explains the professional grower's great care in packing to prevent the roots from drying out during any reasonable delay in transit. His methods of lifting and dispatching from the nursery are further examples of his awareness. On most nurseries the usual procedure is not to lift more trees than can be handled in one day, and when things do not quite work out as intended, any trees left over are usually plunged into sand-pits specially constructed for the purpose. A moral contained in the foregoing remarks is to buy direct from a bona-fide grower, and not from stalls and such-like places, where the roots have been left unprotected.

**Heeling-in**  Roses can be planted at any time from the end of October until the beginning of April, but if, as so often happens, the weather does not permit immediate permanent planting on arrival, the best plan is to plant them temporarily or 'heel' them in. One can prepare for this by digging a trench in an odd corner of the garden so that the unpacking of the bundle and the heeling-in is only a matter of a few minutes' work. The soil taken from the trench should be covered so that dry soil is available for filling in, making the job a comparatively clean one even in wet weather. The trees should be heeled-in separately in a single row, the roots well covered and the soil trodden down hard round them. They are put in separately to enable any given number to be taken without disturbing the remainder. If the trees arrive during a dry period a little common sense in regard to the use of dry soil is necessary, the object of all the precautions outlined being to keep the roots moist.

If an unfortunate delay does occur and the trees on being unpacked have a shrivelled, dry look, bury them completely for about a fortnight. This treatment will plump them up and take away the shrivelled appearance. Whether or not this is necessary, it is a good plan to puddle the roots in a mixture of soil and water immediately before planting.

**The Right Depth to Plant**  When the tree is planted at the right depth, the union should be just below the surface. The 'union' is where the cultivated rose has been budded and joined to the understock and the point from which the top growth begins. If the union is an inch or two either above or below the soil, it will not matter greatly, but it is a common fault, and usually a fatal one, to put the roots down in the soil to a depth where they cannot breathe. The reason for having the union just below the surface of the soil is so that the soil will afford a little protection from frost. In extremely frosty weather the precaution can also be taken of drawing up the soil

15

round the stems, as one does with potatoes, but this extra soil must be levelled off in early spring. This is a common practice in countries where the temperature drops very low, but it is rarely necessary in this country. Owing to the mildness of many of our winters, the risk can be safely taken of planting with the union out of the ground, but, nevertheless, the risk still remains.

**Preparing the Planting Hole** Having settled the depth of planting, the next step is to dig out a hole approximately 12 inches square by 9 inches deep to take the plant. Dust the hole with a small handful of bonemeal

2. *Planting.*
*Spread out roots*
*and carefully fill*
*in with friable*
*soil so as not to*
*leave any air-*
*pockets. Subse-*
*quently prune*
*as indicated.*

and spread out the roots to cover as large an area as possible. Begin to fill in the soil, firming it every now and again until the hole is three parts filled, then tread it down lightly. If the tree sinks a little in so doing, then ease it up and firm again. Replace the remainder of the soil to the bed level, and finish off by treading hard. The main considerations are firm planting and the avoidance of air-pockets round the roots, and if the soil is not sufficiently fine to ensure the latter, it is a good plan to get some friable soil with which peat has been mixed for covering the roots; the soil from the bed can then be used for the remaining filling in. Planting is simple, but if done properly will save a lot of trouble later. By following the procedure given, it should ensure the roots being well covered with none pointing upwards, thus eliminating the risk of their coming up at a distance from the tree and turning into sucker growths.

Climbers, ramblers and climbing Hybrid Teas should all be planted to a similar depth as the bush roses, with the union just below the surface.

**Planting Standard Roses** Standard roses are budded at some distance from the roots, so therefore the union is no guide. Plant them as shallowly as possible. Staking should be done before filling in the soil around the roots. The stake will then be firmer and the risk eliminated of the roots being damaged as they would be if it were driven into the soil after planting.

The stake should be of sufficient length to support the head of the standard, i.e. it should reach to about 1 inch

3. *A rose stand-ard properly staked.*

below the point of budding. Short stakes are worse than no stakes, as unequal pressure is created at the point where they terminate, resulting very often in the breaking of the stem.

**Filling Gaps**  When filling in gaps in established beds, it must be borne in mind that a considerable amount of nutriment has already been taken out of the soil, and also that the cause of the failure of the original plant might still persist. It is therefore most desirable that the old soil should be replaced with fresh. Dig out about a cubic foot of the old soil, and if a little decayed manure is available, mix it with the new soil when filling in. The precaution can always be taken, if the manure is not sufficiently decayed, of covering the roots with unmanured soil to prevent any possible harm.

**Transplanting** The best time to transplant roses is at the end of October, although it can be done with normal precautions at any time from October until April during open weather. The necessity sometimes arises, however, for transplanting to be done out of season, for example, when one moves to another house, say at mid-summer. It can be done quite successfully even at this unfavourable time, provided every precaution is taken to keep the roots moist until they are replanted, and the trees afterwards cared for until they have had time to re-establish themselves. Wet sacks to wrap round the roots are perhaps best for keeping the roots moist, and there is no need to lift the trees with a ball of soil, the roots in any case having to produce fresh rootlets. Avoidance of unnecessary delay is essential, and before planting strip the trees of all leaves; also trim away any damaged roots. Next puddle the roots in a mixture of soil and water and proceed with the planting. Do not prune back the top growths immediately, but wait until the trees begin to break afresh and then prune away any dead parts. See that plenty of water is given to the roots during the first critical weeks after replanting, and it is a good plan to combine with this the syringeing of the stems with clean water two or three times a week until the new growth is forced. The moisture absorbed by the stems will be most helpful in retaining life while the new rootlets are being formed.

# CHAPTER FOUR

# GENERAL CULTIVATION

ROSES in established beds only require one good annual feed of organic matter, and the time to give this is in the spring. It is both wrong and wasteful to apply it in the autumn. Wrong because it holds moisture which is already plentiful at this time of the year, and wasteful because the trees are dormant throughout the winter months and incapable of taking up nourishment. Furthermore, by the spring when they do start into growth most of the food will have been washed out of the manure.

**Liming** Lime improves the condition of the soil and hastens the decomposition of organic matter. Without enough lime in the soil, no rose can possibly make healthy growth, and where the soil is known to be deficient, as heavy and old garden soils often are, an annual dressing in November of carbonate of lime at the rate of 4 ounces to the square yard is very beneficial. If there is any doubt about the necessity of liming, test the soil with hydrochloric acid as mentioned on page 8. With soils containing sufficient calcium, an autumn dressing of basic slag at the rate of 5 ounces to the square yard is to be preferred. It is a safe and slow-acting chemical, providing both lime and phosphates; a separate application of lime is unnecessary.

**Spring Feeding** For the spring feeding of organic matter, horse or farmyard manures are to be preferred, but as these are not always easy to obtain, it is often necessary to use a chemical fertilizer. The latter should not be used, however, without some organic matter to provide bulk to assist in aeration of the soil. Compost or leaf-mould are excellent substitutes, but possibly peat is the most easily obtained. It is low in manurial value itself, but it is excellent for use with the chemicals. Dress with peat after pruning to a depth not exceeding 2 inches, and then apply the chemicals made up as below at the rate of 4 ounces to the square yard, and very lightly fork over.

| | |
|---|---|
| Nitrate of potash | 10 parts by weight. |
| Superphosphate of lime | 12 parts by weight. |
| Sulphate of lime | 8 parts by weight. |
| Sulphate of magnesium | 2 parts by weight. |
| Sulphate of iron | 1 part by weight. |

I emphasize light forking because many gardeners with more zeal than discretion fork over the rose-beds in early spring. They plunge the fork into the soil to the full depth of the tines, in and round the roses, and in turning over the soil break off the hair-like rootlets by which the trees take up nourishment, thus setting back the tree and doing far more harm than good. This breaking off of the rootlets is one of the reasons for subsequent poor growth. It is quite sufficient to prick over the top 2 inches of soil at the end of the year.

**Watering** Except in long periods of drought, it is best not to water, but if it should prove necessary, the best way of doing it is through flower-pots sunk here and there in the beds to their full depth. The quantity needed will depend a great deal on the soil, but usually half a gallon of water to each tree once a week should be ample. With climbers on walls, where the soil is always inclined to be dry, this method of watering is by far the best. The water goes directly to where it is wanted and is not wasted by evaporation.

Much can be done to save watering by preventing evaporation, and this is accomplished by the regular use of the hoe. Drawing the hoe to and fro through the soil seals the many channels through which moisture from below is brought to the surface by capillary action.

The trees also benefit greatly from being syringed with plain water. Moisture taken up by the foliage and stems relieves the strain on the root system, in addition to aiding the foliage itself during hot, dry periods. Incidentally, in most cases of premature defoliation, plain water would do more good than the proprietary sprays so often resorted to. All syringeing should be done in the evening and not in the bright sunshine, otherwise scorching of the foliage is bound to occur.

**Cutting Roses**  The amount of stem to take when cutting rose blooms also often arises. With newly planted trees it is obviously harmful to cut away too much of the new growth; on the other hand, a well-grown, established tree no doubt benefits from a reasonable amount of its growth being cut away, which is equivalent to summer thinning. If in doubt, consider the size of the plant; if plenty of foliage will be left, then do not hesitate to take as long a stem as is needed.

**Removing Dead Wood and Suckers**  Dead wood should

be cut from the tree as soon as it is noticed irrespective of the time of the year, as no purpose is served by leaving it. Other harmful growth is sucker growth, and this, too, should be removed immediately. There is often doubt as to whether or not a particular growth is a sucker. It cannot be determined by the fact that there are seven leaflets, as is sometimes thought, as many varieties throw foliage with both five and seven leaflets. The only certain way is to trace back the growth to its point of origin. If it comes from below the union of the rose and understock it is a sucker, but if above the union it is the rose

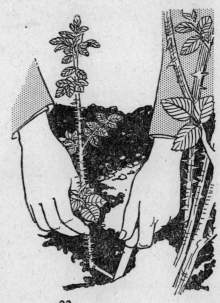

*4. Sucker growth. Remove all sucker growths entirely at their source of origin.*

and must be left. Sucker growths should be cut away in their entirety; it is not sufficient to cut them off at ground level, they should be traced right back to their source, although this may sometimes mean the removal of soil from around the roots. Sucker growths from the stems of standard roses are easily distinguished, but it is surprising how often they are left. Is it from lack of knowledge or just neglect? If from lack of knowledge, all that has to be remembered is that no growths should be permitted between the roots and the head of the plant where the stem has been budded. Any that do appear remove immediately.

Pruning is a subject on its own, and is dealt with in Chapter Five.

# PRUNING

**Why We Prune**  The pruning of roses presents a deal of difficulty to some, but if it is realized that the main object is simply to aid the natural habit of the plant by cutting away weakly and decayed wood, it will perhaps lose some of its complexity. To illustrate this point, as all will have observed, a rose-tree does not grow telescopically; in other words, it does not send out, say 18 inches of growth this year, and the stems carry on extending the following year for another 18 inches. What happens is, in the spring the tree breaks into growth, and in a matter of from 10 to 17 weeks, according to the nature of the variety, the individual stems have reached their limit of growth and then flower. Almost immediately new growths break out from lower down these particular stems, and in their turn, after flowering, they possibly send out further new growths. From this it is obvious that in each instance the new growths must be taking some of the nourishment which would otherwise go to the older ones, with the result that the latter owing to starvation have a tendency to die back. It does not necessarily follow that this will happen immediately, but it is ultimately inevitable. The object of pruning is to aid the tree by cutting away those upper portions of the stems which, having fulfilled their purpose, are no longer required, thus diverting nutriment otherwise wasted to the formation of new, sturdy growth.

The same principle applies to the cutting away of unripe or damaged wood, which takes away nourishment required by the healthy parts of the tree and is, therefore, best dispensed with. Unripeness can be due to a number of causes, but damp, sunless weather in the autumn is possibly the most common reason. Over-feeding through the wrongful application of nitrogenous manure late in the year and the effects of premature defoliation due to disease are further causes.

**Testing for Ripeness** At the time of pruning, to ascertain whether the wood is ripe or not, pinch it hard between the finger and thumb, and if it gives it is soft and no good. Another method is to press the prickles on the stem gently with the thumb. If the wood is ripe they will fly off, but if not they will bend and only break off with great difficulty. One further guide is that the pith of unripe or damaged wood is discoloured. It should be a greeny white, not yellowish or brown.

**When to Prune** What is the best time to prune? There is considerable controversy on this point, some arguing that it can be done as early as December, while others advocate March. Faults to be found with December pruning are, firstly, that in most instances it becomes simply the shortening of the long stems and is, therefore, more in the nature of a tidying up than an actual pruning operation; secondly, the trees carry into the next season new growths made during a spell of mild weather during the winter months, together with prematurely formed foliage. Such foliage is almost certain to be undersized owing to its appearance before the sap is flowing strongly, and damaged as well, as it is rare that the winter ends without a final burst of bad weather. Consequently the trees are inclined to shed their leaves in early summer, thus possibly contributing to attacks from disease. One more point, December pruning, for the foregoing reasons, conflicts with the axiom so often quoted that the trees in the spring should always be cut to a dormant eye.

Now for the other side of the argument. Spring pruning cannot in any way protect the new shoots from the action of late frosts, therefore those in favour of early pruning have a point in their favour. Another risk of March pruning is that in an early season roses pruned at this time are likely to bleed and the trees thus debilitated from loss of sap.

It would seem that weighing all things in the balance, it is best to prune some time towards the end of February. This will be early enough to prune to a dormant eye, also it will avoid the risk of bleeding and yet be late enough to see the effects of the winter on the wood. Although February pruning cannot eliminate the risk of subsequent damage, it will at least restrict it to these late periods. The trees will not start off carrying a number of shoots certain to have been damaged by frost.

**To Prune Hard or Lightly?**　Whether to prune hard or lightly is another question which is often put. Bearing in mind what has been said about the object of pruning, this point largely answers itself. There is no purpose in pruning harder than is warranted. Each tree should be judged

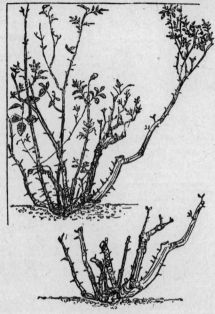

5. *Pruning an established tree.*

on its merits, and the individual stems pruned according to their condition, keeping in mind, however, the general appearance of the tree. Aim to obtain a shapely bush and, whenever possible, prune to an outward pointing eye. The cut itself should be made approximately $\frac{1}{4}$ inch above the eye with a gentle slant in the direction in which it is pointing.

**Strong-growing Roses** The foregoing has dealt with pruning in a general sense, but with strong-growing bushes as, for example, the species Hybrid Musks and those of the Floribunda type, a little licence is permissible, so as to make them flower all the way up and not simply at the top. The way to do this is to retain some of the sturdy stems almost full length, but purposely reduce others to half their length, while yet others should be pruned even lower. This is in no way departing from the general principles advocated, as only the sound, ripe, undamaged growths would be retained full length, those shortened being respectively in their second and third years of growth.

**Standard Roses** The pruning of these trees differs in

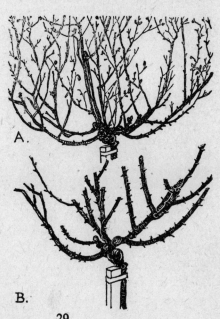

6. *Pruning a standard rose. A, A well-developed head. B, Showing moderate pruning.*

principle in no way from that of their bush counterparts. Retain as much as possible of all good, sound wood, and cut away all weakly, old and damaged growth.

**Ramblers and Climbers** Broadly speaking, these come into two categories, those that throw up a number of supple growths from the base each year, i.e. the Wichuraiana ramblers, and those which do not so freely produce new basal growths, the Wichuraiana climbers, large-flowered climbers and climbing Hybrid Teas. The growths of the latter are usually thick and sturdy, and for this reason are easily distinguishable from the other type. The varieties which produce a large number of supple growths are summer flowering only, and the time to prune them is in September. All the old growths should be cut clean away from the base to make room for the new.

The other type requires little pruning of the main stems beyond thinning them out every now and again by removing the oldest shoots. If it is found that new, vigorous growths have started out from various points along the old stem, prune away as much of the old stem as possible, although at times if the plant is getting overcrowded it is necessary to sacrifice these new growths and remove the old stem entirely. In this second type we get both perpetual flowering varieties, such as the climbing forms of the bush roses, and also varieties that flower but once. However, the foregoing remarks apply to each. The pruning of these should be done in February, and beyond the thinning out referred to nothing more is required beyond the removal of wood that has died back and the shortening of the lateral growths. For pruning purposes, in the list in Chapter Eleven the first type, i.e. those that throw from the base each year a number of supple shoots, have been indicated by Prune 'A', and the second type by Prune 'B'.

**Pruning Newly Planted Roses** Ramblers and climbers of both types are best left unpruned the first year of planting beyond cutting out in February any dead wood. Dwarf bush roses in the first spring of planting should be pruned back fairly hard, i.e. back to within three or four eyes of their base so as to force new basal shoots in order to build up a bushy tree. In poor soils, however, such as that of London, it is best to prune them as lightly as possible, as the food in the old stems will tide the trees over the critical months of April and May until the roots become established. It has been found that in poor soils, where trees do not readily become established and the top growth in consequence dies back, if little wood is left as the result of hard pruning the die-back often reaches the union and kills the tree before the roots have an opportunity of functioning, hence the reason for light pruning. Once the trees have started into growth they can be gone over and any dead wood removed.

During the four to six weeks after the trees have broken into growth, it is necessary to examine periodically the new shoots for frost damage. When this happens, the eye will normally break afresh if damaged early, and two or three growths will come from the one eye. If all of these are left the result will be a number of spindly growths, which is not to be desired, therefore rub out the

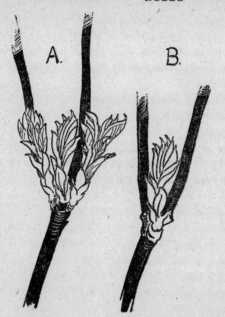

7. A, *The result of frost action —three shoots breaking from one eye.* B, *Excess shoots thinned out, leaving one from each eye.*

surplus shoots so that only one is left from each eye. When the shoot is some 2 inches or more long when frost damage occurs, the only thing to do is to watch the individual shoots, and if they do not grow on but remain weakly, removed them entirely. Unless the frost, however, is very severe they normally recover from the damage, although many will come blind.

# CHAPTER SIX

# ROSE PESTS AND DISEASES

**The Importance of Good Cultivation** In controlling pest and diseases good cultivation is most important, as the maintenance of good health in plants greatly reduces the possibility of attacks. Good cultivation includes the thorough preparation of the soil at the outset, subsequent adequate manuring, but not over-manuring, and the continuous use of the hoe. It does not embrace the frequent application of the hundred-and-one fertilizers offered on the market. As I have said before, one good annual mulching with well-decayed manure in the spring is all that is needed by established roses, unless blooms are required for special purposes, when the risk of the effects of over-feeding is deliberately taken.

**Spraying** The second point is in regard to spraying and

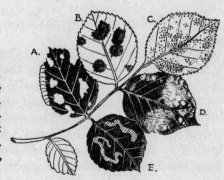

8. *Pests and diseases of the rose.* A, *Leaf-eating caterpillar.* B, *Black spot.* C, *Rust.* D, *Mildew.* E, *Leaf-miner.*

the importance of seeing it is well done, together with a little knowledge of whether one is spraying against fungus disease or pests, and if the latter which kind of pest. It is not possible to outline all the various types of damage which come under the two categories, but where disease is concerned there are certain characteristics which indicate the particular trouble. The three main diseases which affect roses are mildew, rust and black spot, and these and their cures are described on pages 37–41.

In regard to insect pests there are two kinds, sucking-mouthed and biting-mouthed insects. With the first it is necessary to apply a contact wash to block up the breathing pores, and with the second a poisonous cover wash.

The insect pests in their respective categories are:

Sucking-mouthed insects:
*aphides, leaf-hoppers, capsid bugs, thrips and scurfy scale insects*

Biting-mouthed insects:
*leaf-miners, stem and shoot borers, earwigs, caterpillars, chafers, sawflies, slugworms, weevils, etc.*

All spraying must be done in the cool of the evening, as if the sprays are applied in bright sunlight damage to foliage is certain to result. The disease or pest must be tackled early. For example, greenfly, the most common insect pest, can do great harm if allowed to multiply, and it does multiply at an alarming rate, whereas if tackled early it is extremely easy to control. Ordinary soapy water and even clear water is an effective deterrent, and

9. A, *Rose aphis
—greenfly. Keep
pest in check by
killing between
forefinger a n d
thumb and by
spraying with
suitable insecti-
cide.*
B, *A b l o o m
d a m a g e d by
thrips (see be-
low for suitable
sprays).*

trees can be kept quite clean from this pest and a number
of other insects if syringed regularly. There is a number
of excellent and effective proprietary washes on the
market. If one of these is used care must be taken to see
that it reaches every part of the bush, and a heavy wash-
ing until the leaves drip is essential. Against the leaf-
devouring insects, the cover wash should be applied in
a mist-like form so that a fine coating of poison covers
the leaves.

**Spraying against Sucking-mouthed Insects** Effective
home-made washes for sucking-mouthed insects are:

(1) Soft soap and quassia made as follows:

| | | | |
|---|---|---|---|
| *soft soap* | . | . | . | $\frac{1}{4}$ *lb.* |
| *quassia* | . | . | . | 1 *lb.* |
| *water* | . | . | . | 10 *gallons* |

Steep the quassia chips in a quantity of cold water for 12 hours, pour off the extract into the soap solution and make up to 10 gallons. As the quassia is only extracted gradually, the same chips may be steeped several times.

(2) Nicotine wash:

| | | | |
|---|---|---|---|
| *nicotine* (90 *per cent.*) | | | $\frac{1}{4}$ *to* 1 *oz.* |
| *soft soap* | . | . | . | 2 *oz.* |
| *water* | . | . | . | 10 *gallons* |

The soft soap is dissolved in warm water, and when cool the nicotine is stirred into it and the solution made up to the desired quantity.

**Spraying against Biting-mouthed Insects** For biting-mouthed insects arsenate of lead is very effective, and is mixed up as follows:

| | | | |
|---|---|---|---|
| *arsenate of lead* | . | . | $3\frac{1}{2}$ *oz.* |
| *acetate of soda* | . | . | 7 *oz.* |
| *water* | . | . | . | 10 *gallons* |

The arsenate and acetate are dissolved separately in 5 gallons of water and the solutions then mixed together. This wash is also obtainable ready made in paste or powder form. There are also many other effective proprietary insecticides available.

## PESTS

**Thrips** This pest, also known as the thunder-fly, is a serious menace both under glass and in the open garden, especially during hot, dry summers. The flies swarm over all parts of the tree, distorting the young tender shoots; they suck the chlorophyll out of the leaves and, by burrowing into the heart of the buds, cause the malformation of the bloom.

DDT as a spray or dust is most effective, but as a precaution against the malformation of buds it must be used immediately the buds begin to form to prevent the insects from getting into the bloom, where they are safe. Varieties of the Ophelia family are very prone to attack.

**Ants** Although normally looked upon simply as a nuisance, ants can cause the death of trees by making air pockets round the roots with their nest and runs.

If greenfly and other aphides are destroyed, it will reduce the nuisance of the ants swarming over the plants. It is better, however, to destroy their nests with carbon disulphide. Make a number of holes in the soil where the ants are known to be present, and pour into each hole about ⅓ of a fluid ounce of the liquid. Then close the holes to conserve the fumes. Take care not to pour the liquid directly on to the roots.

## DISEASES AND DISORDERS

**Mildew** The first symptom of this disease is that the young growths take on a reddish tinge and start to curl; then as the disease develops they become covered with a whitish powder. Fortunately this early stage is easily corrected. An effective spray is ordinary washing-soda at the rate of 1 ounce to 1 gallon of water, or alternatively the whitish covering can be sponged away with a little warm water. It is important to tackle it early, as if neglected it will get progressively worse, spreading from the foliage to the flowers and stems, spoiling the first and distorting the second. A bad attack will also be carried through the winter months on the stems, completely spoiling the following season's growth and flowering. When this occurs the only thing that can be done is to prune hard in the spring so cutting away the diseased wood. Afterwards the new growth should be closely watched and sprayed at the first sign of recurrence of the disease. A copper white-oil emulsion spray is preferable in bad attacks to the washing-soda solution.

There is no doubt the disease is due to unfavourable weather, hot days followed by cold nights being most conducive to the disease, but poor cultivation, dryness of the roots of the trees, draughty situations and closed-in gardens where the air is stagnant also contribute to its development. The weather conditions referred to are common in the autumn, and as a result it is then that the roses are most often attacked. The tendency is to ignore it so late in the season, but it is not wise to do so, and, after all, washing-soda is inexpensive!

**Rust** This is probably the most dangerous of all rose diseases. It first appears in the spring, but to the unscientific eye it is not recognizable until early summer, when it takes the form of individual reddish-orange patches resembling mustard, on the underside of the leaves. These spores turn blackish in the autumn. The disease very quickly spreads from the foliage to the stems, causing canker of the stems and early defoliation. Spray immediately at the first appearance of the disease with copper white-oil emulsion, repeating every ten days until the trouble is cleared up. Take care to see the spray reaches the fungus on the undersides of the leaves. As a precautionary measure against recurrence of the disease the following year, in the autumn collect all fallen leaves and those remaining on the plant and burn them. Also cut out any cankered stems. Spray in January with copper sulphate at the rate of 1 ounce to a gallon of water, taking care to saturate well both trees and surrounding soil. As the disease is contagious, it is advisable, if only an odd tree is affected, to dig it up and burn it.

A further precaution against recurrence is to cover the rose-beds in the summer with an organic dressing. The value of this is three-fold: it will provide nourishment, protect the roots from the heat of the sun, and act as a buffer between any spores that may be in the soil on diseased foliage from being splashed up on to the trees and starting re-infection. Peat, compost, dung, leaf-mould or grass mowings can be used, either separately or mixed, at a depth not exceeding 2 inches, and it can be maintained at this level throughout the summer with additional grass mowings.

**Black Spot**   This is very common, but fortunately rarely fatal if measures are taken to mitigate its effects.

The first signs are minute black spots on the leaves.

Unless these are checked in their early stage, they rapidly enlarge until each leaf has its entire nutriment absorbed, when it yellows and falls from the tree. Normally the disease does not appear until August or September, but trying weather conditions can cause an earlier attack. Cold winds in late May or early June which upset the normal function of the foliage render it susceptible to the disease, and if hot, wet weather is then experienced an attack is very possible. The use of a colloidal copper spray when the spots first appear will prevent the disease spreading, but if defoliation should occur syringeing with clean water in lieu of the spray is likely to have better results. Apply at the same time a handful of Epsom salt (magnesium sulphate) round the roots of each affected tree and water it in. The salts will help to promote the formation of new foliage.

The harmful effect of the premature defoliation is that the stems without foliage fail to ripen, and are therefore unable to withstand the hard winter weather. The full programme of treatment to offset the unripeness of the wood and to prevent a recurrence of the disease the following year is as follows:

In September apply to the beds a dressing of sulphate of potash at the rate of 3 ounces to the square yard.

In December prune the trees, cutting away all twiggy growth and shortening the long shoots. Strip the trees of any remaining foliage and collect as much as possible of that which has fallen and burn it.

In January spray the trees with copper sulphate at the

rate of 1 ounce to 1 gallon of water, saturating the surrounding soil as well as the trees.

In March complete the pruning, cutting away all wood that has died back and any that is obviously soft.

In April apply a dressing of organic manure.

During the rest of the season, maintain the top dressing as described for rust.

It should be noted, however, that all discoloration of leaves is not caused by black spot; it is very often attributable to other causes, such as mineral deficiencies, cold winds or scorch, the latter due to the action of the sun on wet patches on the leaves. The best advice regarding black spot, should there be any doubt, is first to get it confirmed by a reliable source before starting to spray.

**Chlorosis**   There are several types of chlorosis, but the one common to roses is lime chlorosis, due to an excess of lime in the soil. The leaves gradually lose their green colour and become a sickly yellow, the yellowing usually beginning between the veins. Occasionally some parts of the leaves remain green, and a speckled appearance results.

As it is known that loss of chlorophyll is due to a deficiency of iron, the treatment recommended is the adding of sulphate of iron to the soil at the rate of 1 ounce for each plant. Apply it as crystals about the size of a pea, and lightly prick it in about the roots. Spraying with a solution of 1 ounce of iron sulphate to 1 gallon of water also turns the leaves green, and it is a good plan to combine the two methods.

**Pedicel Necrosis.**   Rotting of blooms on the plant occurs fairly frequently. It can be caused by thrips, or is due to the fact that some full-petalled varieties are apt to ball in a wet season. If the rotting, however, is accompanied by a blackening of the neck of the flower stem, it is fairly certain that the trouble is a physiological one due to a soil deficiency. The most likely deficiency is potassium, and a dressing of sulphate of potash at the rate of 2 ounces to the square yard should rectify matters. Work the potash into the soil, taking care not to disturb the roots of the plants. To hasten recovery spray affected plants every ten days during the growing season with a solution of sulphate of potash at the rate of $1\frac{1}{2}$ ounces to 1 gallon of water until the trouble disappears.

# CHAPTER SEVEN

# PROPAGATION

NEW varieties of rose are raised from seed, but the main method of increasing stock is by budding, which consists of taking a leaf-bud from the cultivated tree and inserting it into an understock. Some trees are also obtained by layering and from striking cuttings, but comparatively few varieties are satisfactory for these methods.

Most cultivated roses are, therefore, parasites living on the nutriment provided by the roots of the wild rose, and this is a sensible arrangement, since they thus benefit from the more vigorous root action of the latter. All who have done a little hybridizing can appreciate the advantage of this arrangement, as they know that the new seedling on its own roots is a puny plant which, more often than not, is so weakly that it dies after its first flowering, the effort being too much for it. Incidentally, it is for this weakness of root action that cultivated roses on their own roots are not successful whether from layering or from cuttings, despite all that has been written advocating these methods of propagation. The only success likely is from varieties which are not too far removed from their original wild state, such as the ramblers, hybrids of species and the hybrid polyantha roses. The modern hybrid tea varieties, with their complicated and heterogeneous pedigrees, are a dismal failure grown in these ways.

**Suitable Stocks from the Hedgerows**  Quite good stocks are to be acquired from cuttings, but if you go to the hedgerows avoid taking them from *R. arvensis*, the white wild rose. Choose them rather from bushes which have

10. *Rose cuttings. The preparation of rose cuttings—showing the bottom cut made immediately below an eye and all foliage removed excepting for that at the top.*

carried deep pink flowers, *R. canina,* the dog brier, which gives far better results. Take the cuttings in October from well-ripened shoots of the current year's growth about the thickness of an average pencil and, after taking out all the eyes from each cutting, with the exception of two at the top, heel them in until February, and then plant them out. They prefer a light sandy soil. The usual length of a cutting is 9 inches, two-thirds of which is inserted in the soil. Its length, however, is not really important, it can be less, but it should still be planted with two-thirds in the ground. The cuttings should be left in their drills for twelve months, and then be transplanted for budding the following summer. Many attempt budding the first summer after planting, before the cutting has made sufficient root action; the take obtained is therefore disappointing, and would-be budders give up in disgust.

**Stocks from Seed** Another method of obtaining stocks is by raising them from seed, but this is an even longer process than striking them from cuttings. The heps are collected when ripe at the end of the year, and the seed extracted and stratified for twelve months before planting. For a small quantity, stratifying is best done by placing the seed in a box of sand out of doors, and turning the sand over from time to time so that the seed is thoroughly weathered. After twelve months of this treatment the seed is sown in drills to a depth of $\frac{1}{2}$ to $\frac{3}{4}$ inch. At the end of the season the seedlings are transplanted. Some will be of sufficient size to bud the following summer, but those that are not will need to be retained for a further twelve months.

If one is prepared to wait, the best course is to obtain a few seedling briers from a nurseryman. Most of the latter take a very broad view of amateurs' budding and will usually supply a few stocks.

**When to Bud** The actual operation of budding can be done from the time the cultivated rose comes into bloom, which in most seasons is June, until the sap in the stocks ceases to flow freely, which is normally some time in September. The earlier the work is done, however, the better. Reference has been made to when the cultivated rose comes into bloom, as it is this factor which governs the start, stems bearing flowers being considered the best from which to take buds, as the flowering ensures ripeness.

**Preparing the Bud** Select good fat buds, preferably those which have not actually broken into growth, and holding the stem, which should have been stripped of its thorns and foliage *but not the leaf stalk,* make a thin cut, starting

11. *Budding.* **A,** *Cutting the bud.* **B,** *Indicating the wood behind the bud which has to be removed.* **C,** *'T' cut in lateral from standard stem.* **D,** *Bud inserted and surplus bark trimmed away.* **E,** *Bud tied in.*

46

$\frac{1}{2}$ inch above the eye to, say, 1 inch below it. The actual distance below is not important, as the bark before inserting has to be trimmed to within $\frac{1}{2}$ inch of the eye. If, however, more bark is taken than is actually required, it will enable the budder to bend the surplus over so that he can get hold of the thin strip of wood lying next to the eye which has to be removed. By holding the bud face downwards between the forefinger and thumb of the left hand, the strip of wood should be eased up with the right hand until it reaches the bud, then a gentle overhand twist away from the body will remove it cleanly. Many seem to have difficulty in doing this, but with a little practice it becomes fairly easy. The alternative is to cut the bud very thinly, and after trimming insert the whole. This is called 'shield budding', and it is reasonably successful, although to remove the wood is better.

**Preparing the Stock**   Prior to preparing the bud make a T-cut about $1\frac{1}{2}$ inches in length, with top cut approximately $\frac{3}{4}$ inch wide, in the neck of the seedling brier, or in a cutting as near to the roots as it is possible to get. Open up the two sides of the cut and then slip in the bud. The leaf stalk which was purposely left will provide the means of handling the bud while this is being done. Push in the bud so that it is neatly enveloped when the bark of the stock is put back into place, trim off the surplus bark of the bud protruding above the cut, and then bind the bud in with raffia. Starting from the bottom, work up, making the tie above the bud. Tie firmly but not too tightly.

This is all that budding consists of. An important tip is not to make a crease in the bark of the bud itself. By careful handling all the creases will have been in the surplus piece of bark which was trimmed away before inserting. If the weather has been dry for a period immediately prior to budding, give the understocks a soaking with water a day or two beforehand to ensure the bark opening well.

Within a month it is possible to tell whether or not the bud has taken. If the piece of bark connected with the eye has turned brown in colour, it has not, and the only thing to do is to try again on the other side of the stock. If budding is commenced early there will be plenty of time to do this.

**After-treatment of Budded Stocks**  In the February following the budding completely remove all the top growth of the understock. With seedling briers the cut should be made $\frac{1}{2}$ inch above the bud, but with cuttings leave a snag of approximately 1 inch. This can be trimmed away later.

It is advisable to stake the new growth when it appears, as during the first season until the union has completely cemented, it is apt to be pulled out by strong winds.

Normally the first growth is checked by frost, and when it breaks a second time more than one shoot appears. If, however, this does not occur naturally, pinch back the new growth when it is about $\frac{1}{2}$ inch in length, and thus force it to break afresh, otherwise the new tree will carry one stem only.

All budding is the same whether for bushes or standards, except that with the latter if *canina* stems (dog brier) are used, the buds are inserted into the two or three lateral growths at the top of the stem, and not into the main stem itself (see below). The buds should be inserted, however, as near to the main stem as possible, so as not to leave room for wild growth to grow out between them and the main stem. With *rugosa* stems, two or three buds are inserted, but these go directly into the main stem at the required height on different sides of the stem.

**Stems for Standards** Dog-brier stems are obtainable from the strong root shoots of *R. canina* in the hedgerows and woods. The best are those about $\frac{3}{4}$ inch in diameter, twelve months old and not those of the current year's growth. The stems present a little difficulty in obtaining, as a portion of the old root with one or two fibrous roots attached is necessary if they are to succeed. It is not sufficient to cut the stems off at ground level. Before planting the stem, if the base terminates in a knobbly lump this should be trimmed, retaining a little of the old root with one or two fibrous roots attached. If the whole of the knob is left, sucker growth will be a nuisance later. Before planting shorten the stem to approximately 4 feet, and take out all eyes up the stem except for two or three at the top. These eyes will break in the spring, and the laterals they provide will be of sufficient size to bud by the summer.

**Layering** This consists in bending over a growing shoot from a tree in March, slitting it some 6 to 9 inches from its end and pegging the piece down. Care should be taken not to sever it completely, as while it is still attached a certain amount of nourishment will be supplied from the main stem. By the autumn the piece layered will have rooted and it can then be completely severed.

# CHAPTER EIGHT

# EXHIBITING

**Staging**  Watch some of the old hands at the game. Assimilate first the cool, methodical way they go about their work. Their first consideration is to unpack their roses and get them into water. Then they find their classes; perhaps in so doing casting an eye over the blooms being staged by competitors, but undaunted by anything they

12. *Three specimen blooms in a vase, indicating the advantage of good arrangement.*

see, they quietly get to work. From the study of the schedule before setting out, they know more or less to which class each bloom is allocated, and to facilitate the arranging each is labelled. Possibly, too, they have drawn up a list for reference of the names of the roses for the respective classes. How gently and lovingly they handle their blooms, and how careful they are not to leave any out of water. One of the greatest mistakes made by the novice is to paw over the blooms, leaving them to dry out on the staging while examining others until, by the time the blooms are eventually staged, they have lost most of their freshness.

**Dressing** Watch, too, how the old hand dresses a bloom. First he will trim away with a pair of scissors any damaged guard petals, and then with the forefinger and thumb gently bend over the outer petals so that the more intense inner colouring of the bloom is revealed. This dressing, however, is an art only to be acquired from practice, as the tendency is to overdo it, thus altering the character of the bloom, rendering it, for this reason, liable to disqualification.

**Arranging the Finished Exhibit** Finally, note the perfection of their completed exhibits. In a box class, the colours will be arranged harmoniously with the largest blooms in the top row and the smallest in the right-hand corner and, in a vase each bloom will stand out, making as much of itself as possible. They will not all have been rammed down into the vase so that one bloom partially conceals another.

These are a few of the pointers to be picked up quickly

13. *Exhibiting. A well-arranged box of six specimen blooms.*

by exhibiting one's own roses, provided a little study and observation accompany the effort.

**Preparations Before the Show** The first essential of successful exhibiting is the production of good blooms, which demands good cultivation. The next important point is to grow the right type of bloom for whatever object is in view. The lists in Chapter Ten will be helpful.

The best results are obtained from growing a number of trees of a few varieties, rather than spreading the quantity over a greater number of varieties. If one has a dozen plants of, say, Ena Harkness, it is more possible on a given date to cut half a dozen good blooms from them than it would be if one had a dozen different varieties, as all the trees of Ena Harkness would be in bloom about the same time, whereas the flowering period of the dozen different varieties might be spread over several weeks. Where large quantities are grown this point loses some of its force, but where space is limited it is important.

**Pruning for Exhibition**   There is no need to prune roses harder for exhibition than for general cultivation, but it

14. *Disbudding. A, Clusters of buds. B, Showing extent of disbudding for the production of specimen blooms.*

53

is important to go over the trees, rubbing out unwanted shoots, leaving one stem only from each eye. These stems should be disbudded later to two buds if the object is a large specimen bloom from each. It is advisable to leave two buds in case of accident or damage to one of them. Should the plants be decorative varieties of the Hybrid Tea type reduce the number judiciously. It is not possible to lay down a hard-and-fast rule on this point, as the number of buds varies according to the variety.

**Feeding** As soon as the buds are formed start liquid feeding. A suitable mixture is made by steeping a bag of manure in a tub of water. The liquid should be diluted to a pale straw colour at the time of application and given weekly at the rate of 1 gallon per tree. Feeding should not be continued after the end of July, as it produces soft wood which will not winter well unless given the opportunity of hardening off. In early September apply to the beds a dressing of sulphate of potash at the rate of 2 ounces to the square yard to assist this process.

**Retarding Blooms** Nothing can be done to hasten blooming, but blooms can be retarded by using shades. These are cones made from calico stretched over wire. The value of shading is three-fold: it permits the bloom to develop at a slower rate, shields it from the bleaching effects of the sun and provides protection from the rain. Shading, in conjunction with tying the centre of the bloom with a strand of thick wool for a couple of days prior to the show, increases the size of the petals, and for this reason is a practice adopted by exhibitors. The tying,

*15. A specimen bloom, showing 'tie' with
thick, soft wool.*

however, is not an unmixed blessing, as when the ties are
removed at the show the blooms are apt to blow quickly.
It is far easier to gauge the lasting qualities of a bloom
that has been grown naturally.

CHAPTER NINE

# CLASSIFICATION

HOW often the remark is passed, 'I do like tea roses', and when the speaker is pressed as to why the reference to 'tea' roses, it is found that he or she has a hazy notion that all yellow roses are tea roses. Another believes the term applies to pink roses, whereas in point of fact they are a distinct class embracing all colours, reds, pinks, yellows, apricots, blush, etc., etc. Very few 'teas', however, are now grown, as the class has been almost completely swallowed up by the Hybrid Tea roses, which were evolved by the crossing of this class with the Hybrid Perpetual roses some fifty years or so ago. The Hybrid Teas are usually listed as H.Ts., which together with (T.) for Tea and (H.P.) for Hybrid Perpetual are examples of the various symbols seen in catalogues and books of roses. These symbols are a mystery to newcomers to rose growing, although, without going too deeply into the subject, it is possible to explain them broadly.

The logical beginning is with the native wild roses of the different countries, the species roses. The self seedlings from these are sub-species, and the cultivated crossings of the different species, hybrids of the species. All the foregoing bear a botanical name, which is generally indicative of the country of origin, such as *R. chinensis, R. virginia, R. gallica,* or descriptive of the plant, heps or blooms, e.g. *R. spinosissima, R. pomifera* and *R. mul-*

56

*tiflora*. Species discovered during the last century or so, together with a few others the result of hybridization, often bear a derivation of the name of the discoverer or the hybridist, e.g. *R. Banksiae, R. Bakeri, R. Brunonii*. In each instance the prefix *R.* for rosa is given to indicate the genus.

The following symbols, although not a complete list, are those in common usage:

**Ayr (Ayrshire)**  A group of hardy climbing roses derived from *R. arvensis*, a native species of this country.

**B. (Bourbon)**  A group which originally came from the Isle of Bourbon, believed to be a cross between *R. chinensis* and *R. gallica*.

**C. (China)**  Varieties derived from the species *R. indica* (the Chinese rose) and the pioneer of the autumn-flowering roses.

**D. (Damask)**  As the name indicates, this is a native of Syria. Remarkable for its delicious scent.

**H.B. (Hybrid Bourbon)**  A descendant from the French and Provence roses.

**H.N. (Hybrid Noisette)**  So named after the raiser, an American, M. Philippe Noisette, and obtained by the fertilization of *R. moschata,* the Musk Rose, with the Common Blush China, *R. indica*. Crossed with the Tea Rose and later merged into that group, i.e. the Teas.

**H.P. (Hybrid Perpetual)**  The result obtained by crossing the Damask Perpetual with the Bourbon and Chinese rose, *R. indica*. Although so named, many varieties of this group were summer flowering only.

**Hy. Poly. (Hybrid Polyantha)**  A new class derived

16. *The form of typical Flori-bunda roses.*

from crossing the dwarf polyantha roses with the hybrid tea roses. First introduced by the Danish hybridist D. T. Poulsen in 1924 as a result of crossing the Orleans Rose (Poly.) and Red Star (H.T.) to which he gave the name Else Poulsen. Others bearing the Poulsen name came in quick succession, Kirsten Poulsen, Karen Poulsen, Poulsen's Pink, Poulsen's Yellow, etc., which became generally known as the Poulsen roses. Their particular charm is that they are easy to grow and bear large clusters of flowers from early June until late in the autumn, and for these reasons have achieved great popularity. During the last few years other hybridists working on the class have introduced other blood into the type, such as the Sweet Brier and Musk strains, so much so that few now have any polyantha blood in them, and despite the comparative newness of the classification (Hy. Poly.) the National Rose Society has provisionally given them the omnibus term Floribunda, although still classifying the Hybrid Polyanthas under this heading, where such parentage is known.

**H.S.B. (Hybrid Sweet Brier)**   A class of roses raised by the late Lord Penzance at the end of the nineteenth century. They are believed to be the result of crossing *R. rubiginosa* (sweet brier) with the Hybrid Perpetuals. The perfume of the foliage which is a characteristic of the original species persists in its hybrids.

**H.T. (Hybrid Tea)**   This group is now the main one; in it have been merged the Hybrid Perpetuals, Teas and Pernetianas. The fullness of bloom of the Hybrid Perpetual, the delicacy and shapeliness of the Teas, and the wide range of colouring introduced by the Pernetianas are all blended in the lovely garden specimens of the present day.

**Pern. (Pernetiana)**   A class of perpetual flowering roses raised by and named after M. Pernet Ducher of Lyons. The first of this class, Soleil d'Or, made its appearance in 1900. Their merit was in the distinctive shade of yellow that pervaded all the varieties, due to their origin in part to *R. lutea* (the Austrian brier). As previously stated, this class is now merged in the Hybrid Teas.

**Poly. (Polyantha)**   This class is related to the species

17. *The form of typical Hybrid Tea roses.*

*R. multiflora,* but has a dwarf habit of growth. The original varieties are thought to be a cross between the species and a tea-scented variety. Two of the earliest, Perle d'Or and Cécile Brünner, are still in existence. Their distinctive feature is the perfection of the very miniature blooms which are produced in sprays. Since the advent of the more vigorous Hybrid Polyanthas, the class is gradually becoming extinct.

**Prov. (Provence)**   This group is a native of the South of France and named after the province. The original species is *Rosa centifolia,* the parent of the cabbage roses.

**Rug. (rugosa)**  The rose of Japan, the parent of a distinct class of hybrids. The most striking features of the original species are that its stems are densely covered with sharp, straight-pointed prickles; and the bush in the autumn carries fruits which for a rose are of immense size. Used considerably both as a stem for standard roses and as an understock for dwarf roses.

**T. (Tea)**  This class was so named because its perfume was reminiscent of tea. The original parents, pink and yellow varieties of the family *R. indica odorata*, came from China. The two varieties were married by a Frenchman, whom it is thought also infused the blood of the Bourbon rose into the subsequent crossings. The class as a whole was rather tender, although there are one or two exceptions, such as Gloire de Dijon, which for this reason is still in cultivation. With the advent of the Hybrid Teas, of which it was one of the parents, the class has now become almost extinct.

**Wich. climb.; Wich. ramb. (Wichuraiana climbers and Wichuraiana ramblers)**  These have been obtained by crossing the wild rose, *R. Wichuraiana*, of China and Japan with the Hybrid Tea, and the resultant offspring with other roses, producing variable results. As the habit of growth of some is different from that of others, it is necessary to group them separately, and details of the distinctive character of growth were given when discussing pruning on page 30.

The foregoing by no means covers all the various groups of roses, but is possibly sufficient to give the newcomer an insight into the progress made with roses over the centuries, and will, it is hoped, enable him to study a rose catalogue with more understanding.

Before concluding this chapter, one further explanation may be helpful in respect of the term 'sport'.

A 'sport' can either be a variation in the colour of the bloom from that of the original, or a climbing sport, when the habit of growth changes from the dwarf to that of the climbing form. With the first it is not always easy to tell, as a change of colour can be a reversion to one of the parents of the original plant. 'Sporting', however, does take place, and two modern roses which are very prone to this habit are McGredy's Sunset, from which quite a number of sports have been obtained, notably Beryl Formby and Flaming Sunset, and Better Times, from which arose Red Better Times, which again sported to produce Modern Times, the striped rose resembling a tulip, which caused quite a sensation at a show in 1952.

The climbing Hybrid Teas come into the category of climbing sports—all are counterparts of their bush varieties, excepting for their climbing habit. What happens is that a bush variety will suddenly throw out a climbing shoot. If after budding from this shoot the climbing habit continues, it is what is termed 'fixed' and another climbing hybrid tea variety is added to the list. It is a natural phenomena and cannot be artificially produced, and this explains why there are not climbing forms of all the hybrid tea bush roses.

# CHAPTER TEN

# SELECTIONS OF ROSES FOR VARIOUS PURPOSES

## ARRANGED IN COLOUR

**Blush and Flesh**

Gordon Eddie

Ophelia

Polly

Suzon Lotthé

**Bicolour Red and Yellow**

Autumn

Charles Gregory

Condesa de Sastago

Fortyniner

Gay Crusader

McGredy's Sunset

Mme L. Dieudonné

President Herbert Hoover

Souvenir Jacques Verschuren

Talisman

**Coppery Rose and Bronze**

Cynthia Brooke

Emma Wright

Lady Belper

Mary Wheatcroft

Mev. G. A. Van Rossem

Mme Kriloff

Mrs Sam McGredy

Pilar Landecho

**Dark Crimson**

Charles Mallerin

Crimson Glory

Dr F. G. Chandler

Étoile de Hollande

Red Ensign

William Harvey

**Light Crimson**

Ena Harkness

Glory of Rome

Hugh Dickson           Poinsettia
Karl Herbst            W. E. Chaplin

**Pink**
Admiral                Monique
Dr Débat               Picture
Lady Sylvia            Shot Silk
Michèle Meilland       Show Girl

**Carmine and Rose**
Applause               Mrs Henry Bowles
Betty Uprichard        Opera
Charlotte Armstrong    Rubáiyát

**White and Cream**
Clarice Goodacre       McGredy's Ivory
Frau Karl Druschki     Mrs Herbert Stevens
Innocence              Virgo

**Yellow**
Fantasia               Mme Yves Latieule
Golden Dawn            Peace
Golden Melody          Phyllis Gold
Grand'mère Jenny       Spek's Yellow
McGredy's Yellow       Sutter's Gold

## ROSES FOR WEEPING STANDARDS

Alberic Barbier        François Juranville
Crimson Shower         Léontine Gervais
Dorothy Perkins        Minnehaha
Excelsa                Sanders White

## ROSES FOR WALLS

**For Walls facing North or East**

Allen Chandler
Felicité et Perpetué
Hugh Dickson
Mermaid

Mme Alfred Carrière
Mme Caroline Testout
  (climbing)
*R. moschata*

**For Walls facing South or West**

Lady Hillingdon (climbing)
Mermaid
Mme Abel Chatenay
  (climbing)
Mme Butterfly (climbing)

Ophelia (climbing)
*R. bracteata* (the Macartney
  Rose)
Shot Silk (climbing)
Zéphirine Drouhin

## ROSES FOR ARCHES AND PERGOLAS

Albertine
Crimson Conquest
Crimson Shower
Dorothy Perkins
Excelsa
Evangeline

François Juranville
Léontine Gervais
Mary Wallace
Sanders White
Thelma

## ROSES FOR LOW HEDGES APPROXIMATELY 3 TO 4 FEET

Dainty Maid
Elmshorn
Else Poulsen
Florence Mary Morse

Frensham
Orange Triumph
Salmon Spray

## ROSES FOR HEDGES APPROXIMATELY 5 FEET AND OVER

Hybrid Musk Cornelia

Hybrid Musk Felicia

Hybrid Musk Penelope
Hybrid Musk Prosperity
R. *alba* Great Maiden's
  Blush
R. *alba* Celestial
R. *alba maxima*
R. *spinosissima*

## VERY FRAGRANT ROSES

Autumn
Charles Mallerin
Christopher Stone
Crimson Glory
Dr F. G. Chandler
Ena Harkness
Étoile de Hollande
Golden Melody
Hector Deane
Hugh Dickson
Lady Sylvia
Lunelle
Mme Butterfly
Monique
Ophelia
Polly
President Hoover
Red Ensign
Rubáiyát
Shot Silk
Sutter's Gold
Talisman
The Doctor
William Harvey

## ROSES FOR EXHIBITION PURPOSES

**Specimen Blooms**

Crimson Glory
Directeur Guèrin
Dr F. G. Chandler
Ellinor Le Grice
Ena Harkness
Glory of Rome
Golden Dawn
Golden Melody
McGredy's Yellow
Peace
Percy Izzard
Phyllis Gold
Red Ensign
Rex Anderson
Sam McGredy
Show Girl

The Doctor  William Moore
William Harvey

## Medium-sized Blooms for Exhibition in the Decorative Classes

Autumn  Mrs Sam McGredy
Charles Gregory  Ophelia
Comtesse Vandal  Picture
Étoile de Hollande  Polly
Hinrich Gaede  President Herbert Hoover
Lady Sylvia  Shot Silk
McGredy's Sunset  Signora
Mme Butterfly  Sir Henry Segrave
Mrs Herbert Stevens  Spek's Yellow

## ROSES FOR SPECIMEN BUSHES

Danaë  *R. alba semiplena*
Elmshorn  *R. Ecae*
Eva  *R. Harrisonii*
Felicia  *R. Hugonis*
Moonlight  *R. Moyesii*
Pax  *R. Moyesii Nevada*
Penelope  *R. rugosa Schneeswerg*
*R. alba maxima*  *R. sericea pteracantha*

## VIGOROUS-GROWING ROSE BUSHES FOR TOWN GARDENS

Admiral  Condesa de Sastago
Autumn  Dainty Maid
Betty Uprichard  Ena Harkness

Étoile de Hollande
Fandango
Frau Karl Druschki
Frensham
Golden Dawn
Grand'mère Jenny

Karl Herbst
Mme Caroline Testout
Orange Triumph
Peace
Show Girl
Violinista Costa

# CHAPTER ELEVEN

# A DESCRIPTIVE LIST OF ROSES

The following explanations of the style of arrangement of the descriptions may be helpful: (1) the name of each rose is given; (2) the class to which it belongs; (3) the raiser's or introducer's name and date of introduction; (4) the parentage, if known; (5) the colour of the flower; (6) its petalage, if known; (7) the character of the growth, whether vigorous, moderate or otherwise; (8) fragrance; (9) pruning reference of climbing and rambling varieties where applicable.

It may also be helpful to explain the terms single, semi-double and full or double in relation to the type of bloom.

By 'single flowered' is meant a bloom having only one row of petals, five in all.

By 'semi-double' is meant a bloom having more than one row of petals, but not more than eighteen petals in all.

By 'full' or 'double' is meant a bloom with full petalage.

**Admiral** (H.T.) A. Dickson & Son, 1949. Coral to salmon pink. Cupped blooms, large, $4\frac{1}{2}$ in. across, 35 petals. Vigorous, $2\frac{1}{2}$ ft. Very fragrant.

**Alain** (Hy. poly.) F. Meilland, 1946. Glowing scarlet

crimson, 2½ in., 24 petals, free flowering in large trusses. Vigorous and upright growth, 2 ft.

**Alberic Barbier** (Wich. ramb.) Barbier, 1900. Yellow buds, changing to creamy white. Very vigorous. Early June flowering. Prune B.

**Albertine** (Wich. ramb.) Barbier, 1921. Coppery chamois, passing to salmon, 26 petals. Very vigorous. Sweetly scented. Mid-June flowering. Prune B.

**Allen Chandler** (Clg. H.T.) Prince, 1924. Vivid scarlet. Semi-double blooms. Vigorous. Prune B.

**American Pillar** (Wich. ramb.) Van Fleet, 1905. Bright rose, white eye. Single flowered. Very vigorous. Early July flowering. Prune B.

**Anne Poulsen** (Hy. poly.) Poulsen, 1935. Bright pink, shaded crimson, 14 petals. Vigorous and upright, 3½ ft. Very fragrant. With light pruning will make large bush.

**Applause** (H.T.) Swim, Armstrong Nurseries, 1950. Contrast × Charlotte Armstrong. Carmine rose. Blooms high centred, large and very double, 50 petals. Vigorous upright growth. 2½ ft. Slight fragrance.

**August Seebauer** (Hy. poly.) W. Kordes, 1950. Else Poulsen × Break o' Day. Pink blooms 3 in. across, produced in trusses, 40 small petals. Vigorous growth, 2 ft. 6 in. Fragrant.

**Autumn** (H.T.) L.B. Coddington, 1930. Orange, shaded pink. Very full shapely blooms, 70 petals. Moderately vigorous, 1½–2 ft. Fragrant.

**Betty Uprichard** (H.T.) A. Dickson & Sons, 1921. Coppery pink shaded salmon, 17 petals. Very vigorous, 3½ ft. Blooms thin and fleeting. Fragrant.

**Bonn** (Hy. moschata) W. Kordes, 1949. Hamburg × Sondermeldung. Orange scarlet. Medium-sized blooms opening to 3 in., 18 petals. Shrub rose, 4 ft. Slight musk fragrance.

**Border King** (Hy. poly.) G. de Ruiter, 1950. Brilliant strawberry red, individually 1 in. across with 17 petals, produced in large clusters. Growth very vigorous, 2 ft.

**Cécile Brünner** (Poly.) Ducher, 1880. Blush shaded pale rose. Very minute perfectly formed blooms. The best of its class. If lightly pruned will make a big bush, 3 ft. Fragrant.

**Chaplin's Pink Climber** (Wich. climber) Chaplin Bros., Ltd., 1929. Carmine pink, 18 petals. Vigorous. Blooms in clusters over a long period. Fragrant. Prune B.

**Charles Gregory** (H.T.) H.A. Verschuren, 1947. Orange and scarlet. Shapely blooms, 25 petals. Vigorous, 2½ ft. A good variety for cut blooms.

**Charles Mallerin** Meilland, 1947. Glory of Rome × Tassin. Velvety crimson. Large blooms of good form, 35 petals. Upright growth, 2–3 ft. Very fragrant.

**Charlotte Armstrong** Lammerts, Armstrong Nurseries, 1950. Soeur Thèrese × Crimson Glory. Carmine shaded orange and pink. Urn-shaped blooms, 30 petals. Growth vigorous, 2 ft. Slight fragrance.

**Christine** (Pern.) S. McGredy & Son, 1918. Deep golden yellow. Blooms small, 30 petals. Moderately vigorous, 1½ ft. Should be planted closely. Unusually free and keeps its colour.

**Christopher Stone** (H.T.) H. Robinson, 1934. Crimson,

shaded velvet. Blooms thin, 21 petals. Vigorous, 2 ft. Fragrant.

**Clarice Goodacre** (H.T.)  A. Dickson & Sons, 1916. Chrome on ivory white. Shapely blooms, 25 petals. Vigorous and bushy, 2 ft. Fragrant.

**Comtesse Vandal** (H.T.) Leenders & Co., 1932. Ophelia × Mrs Aaron Ward × Souv. de Claudius Pernet. Reddish copper, edged pale pink. Long bud, shapely bloom, 30 petals. Vigorous, 2½ ft. Fragrant. A fine rose, but one very subject to mildew.

**Condesa de Sastago** (Pern.) Pedro Dot, 1934. Orange flame, reverse of petals gold. Cup-shaped full blooms, 38 petals. Vigorous and bushy, 2 ft. Fragrant. Very free flowering and lasting.

**Cornelia** (Hy. Musk.) J. H. Pemberton, 1924. Old rose colour. Blooms small, produced in clusters, 40 petals. Vigorous, 4–5 ft. Fragrant. Very hardy and will make a large bush.

**Crimson Conquest** (Wich. climber)  Chaplin Bros., Ltd., 1931. Scarlet. Single flowering. Vigorous climber. Fragrant. Early July flowering. Prune B.

**Crimson Glory** (H.T.) W. Kordes, 1935. Deep velvety crimson. Shapely full blooms, 30 petals. Moderately vigorous. Very fragrant. A beautiful variety that requires good cultivation.

**Crimson Shower** (Wich. ramb.)  A. Norman, 1951. Crimson. Blooms semi-double, 1½ in., across produced in large trusses. Very vigorous. Slight fragrance. Late flowering. Prune A.

**Cynthia Brooke** (H.T.) S. McGredy & Son, 1942.

Apricot yellow. Large globular blooms, 43 petals. Spreading sprawly growth, 1½ to 2 ft. Fragrant.

**Dainty Bess** (H.T.) W. E. B. Archer and Daughter, 1926. Silvery pink. Single blooms. Vigorous, 3–4 ft. A beautiful single-flowered rose, perpetual blooming in clusters.

**Dainty Maid** (Hy. poly) E. B. Le Grice, 1938. Carmine, shaded white. Large semi-double blooms, 8 petals. Very vigorous 3–4 ft. A very fine variety that blooms well into the late autumn. No fragrance.

**Danaë** (Hy. Musk) Rev. J. H. Pemberton, 1913. Soft yellow, 48 petals. Blooms recurrently in clusters. Very vigorous, 6 ft. Musk fragrance.

**De Ruiter's Herald** (Hy. moschata) G. de Ruiter, 1948. Brilliant scarlet shaded orange, small single flowers in very large clusters. Vigorous and upright, 2–3 ft.

**Directeur Guèrin** (H.T.) J. Gaujard, 1937. Creamy yellow, centre golden orange. Large shapely blooms, 38 petals. Vigorous and branching, 2–2½ ft. Fragrant.

**Donald Prior** (Hy. poly.) D. Prior & Son, 1934. Bright scarlet, flushed crimson. Large semi-double blooms carried in small clusters, 11 petals. Vigorous, 3 ft. Fragrant.

**Dorothy Perkins** (Wich. ramb.) Jackson & Perkins, 1901. Rose pink. Blooms small, borne in clusters. Very vigorous. Mid-July flowers. Prune A.

**Dr Débat** (H.T.) F. Meilland, 1948. Radiance × Dame Edith Helen. Soft pink shaded gold at base. Long buds, large and shapely, 30 petals. Vigorous and upright, 3 ft. Fragrant.

**Dr F. G. Chandler** (H.T.)   A. Dickson & Sons, 1938. Velvety crimson. Blooms large, cupped. Moderately vigorous, 1½ ft. Fragrant.

**Dr Van Fleet** (Wich. ramb.)   Van Fleet, 1910. Soft blush. Clusters of soft pink cupped blooms, 34 petals. Very vigorous. Fragrant. Prune A.

**Dusky Maiden** (Hy. poly.)   E. B. Le Grice, 1947. (Daily Mail Scented × Étoile de Hollande) seedling × Else Poulsen. Deep scarlet shaded dark maroon with golden anthers. Large semi-double. Vigorous, 2 ft. Fragrant.

**Easlea's Golden Rambler** (Wich. ramb.)   W. Easlea & Sons, 1932. Golden yellow, splashed red. Large flat blooms, 26 petals. Vigorous. Early July flowering. Blooms from laterals. Fragrant. Prune B.

**Ellinor Le Grice** (H.T.)   E. B. Le Grice, 1949. Lilian × Yellow Crest. Yellow. Blooms large and globular, 35 petals. Vigorous and compact, 1½–2 ft. Fragrant.

**Elmshorn** (Hy. Musk)   Kordes, 1950. Hamburg × Verdun. Deep pink. Blooms small, 1 in., 36 petals, produced in large trusses. Very vigorous, 6 ft. Perpetual flowering. Slight musk fragrance.

**Else Poulsen** (Hy. poly.)   Poulsen, 1924. Bright rose pink. Large, flat, semi-double blooms, 11 petals. Vigorous, 3–4 ft. Susceptible to disease.

**Emily Gray** (Wich. ramb.)   Dr A. H. Williams, 1916. Golden yellow, 19 petals. Very vigorous. Beautiful foliage, almost evergreen. Mid-June flowering. Prune B.

**Emma Wright** (H.T.)   S. McGredy & Son, 1917. Pure orange. Semi-double, flat blooms, nice in bud, 19 petals. Moderately vigorous, 1½–2 ft. Fragrant.

**Ena Harkness** (H.T.)  A. Norman, 1946. Southport ×
Crimson Glory. Scarlet crimson. Shapely full blooms, 36
petals. Freely produced. An outstanding rose. Vigorous,
2 ft. Fragrant.

**Étoile de Hollande** (Clg. H.T.)  Leenders & Co., 1932.
Dark red. A fine sport from the dwarf variety. Prune B.

**Étoile de Hollande** (H.T.)  Verschuren, 1919. Dark red.
Shapely in bud, opening rather loose, 24 petals. Vigorous,
2½ ft. One of the best dark-red roses, but blooms have
weak neck.

**Eva** (Hy. Musk)  W. Kordes, 1937. Dark red, 28 petals.
Very vigorous, 5 ft. Blooms in clusters throughout the
summer and autumn. Fragrant. Requires very little pruning.

**Evangeline** (Wich. ramb.)  M. H. Walsh, 1906. Pale pink
with white centre, 5 petals. Very vigorous. Single-flower-
ing blooms are borne in clusters. Mid-July flowering.
Very fragrant. Prune A.

**Excelsa** (Wich. ramb.)  M. H. Walsh, 1909. Bright rosy
crimson. Small rosette blooms produced in clusters, 35
petals. Vigorous. Mid-July flowering. Prune A.

**Fantasia** (H.T.)  A. Dickson & Sons, 1942. Light yellow
blooms opening flat, 3–4 in. in diameter. Very free flowering. Vigorous, 2 ft. Sweet fragance. A good bedding
variety.

**Fashion** (Hy. poly.)  E. S. Boerner, Jackson & Perkins,
1947. Pinocchio × Crimson Glory. A rich salmon, large-
flowered, 24 petals. Bushy and free flowering, large
clusters. Moderately vigorous, 1 ft. 6 in. to 2 ft.

**Felicia** (Hy. Musk)  J. H. Pemberton, 1928. China pink,

shaded yellow, 35 petals. The blooms are produced in large erect clusters of pretty rosette form. Vigorous, 5 ft. Very fragrant.

**Felicité et Perpetué** (Sempervirens) Jacques, 1827. Pale cream. Blooms fairly large, very double and flat, produced in clusters. Very vigorous. Foliage almost evergreen. Prune B.

**Fellenberg** (C.) Fellenberg, 1857. Rose crimson. Rosette-shaped blooms, 40 petals. Vigorous, 3–4 ft. Fragrant.

**Florence Mary Morse** (Hy. sweet brier) Kordes, 1951. Baby Château × *R. rubiginosa magnifica*. Coppery scarlet. Blooms large, 3 in. across, produced in large trusses, 15 petals. Very vigorous, 3 ft. Slight musk fragrance.

**Fortyniner** (H.T.) Swim, Armstrong Nurseries. Contrast × Charlotte Armstrong. Light crimson, gold reverse. Blooms large, opening rather loose, 30 petals. Vigorous, $2\frac{1}{2}$ ft. No fragrance.

**François Juranville** (Wich. ramb.) Barbier, 1906. Deep fawn pink. Blooms medium size opening flat, double. Very vigorous. Mid-June flowering. Fragrant. Prune A.

**Frau Karl Druschki** (H.P.) P. Lambert, 1900. Pure white. Blooms large and shapely. Very vigorous, 3 ft. Lacks fragrance.

**Frensham** (Hy. poly.) A. Norman, 1946. Hy poly. seedling × Crimson Glory. Deep scarlet. Large semi-double blooms, 3 in. across, produced in large trusses, 12 petals. Very vigorous, 3–4 ft. No fragrance.

**Gay Crusader** (H.T.) H. Robinson, 1948. Phyllis Gold × Catalonia. Outer petals deep yellow, inner orange and scarlet. Blooms large, shapely and high centred, 30 petals. Moderately vigorous, 1½–2 ft. Fragrant.

**Gloire de Dijon** (T.) Jacotot, 1850. Buff or orange yellow. Large full flat blooms. Vigorous climber, for north and east walls. Strong tea perfume.

**Glory of Rome** (H.T.) D. Aicardi, 1937. Dame Edith Helen × Sensation. Colour variable between red and pink, inclined to blue at times. Blooms large and shapely, 50 petals. Very vigorous, 2½–3 ft. Fragrant.

**Golden Dawn** (H.T.) Grant, 1929. Elegante × Ethel Somerset. Pale lemon yellow. Blooms large and full, 45 petals. Vigorous and sprawling, 2 ft. Its fault is that the blooms often show a split centre when three-parts open. Fragrant.

**Golden Melody** (H.T.) La Florida, 1934. Buff yellow. High pointed blooms, 35 petals. Vigorous, 2 ft. Very fragrant.

**Goldilocks** (Hy. poly.) E. S. Boerner, Jackson & Perkins, 1945. Unnamed seedling × Doubloons. Rich yellow double flowers, borne freely in clusters. Moderately vigorous, 1 ft. 6 in. to 2 ft. Fragrant.

**Gordon Eddie** (H.T.) Eddie, 1949. Royal Visit × Cynthia Brooke. Deep apricot in centre with lighter edges. Blooms high pointed and shapely, 40 petals. Vigorous and upright, 2–2½ ft. Fragrant.

**Grand'mère Jenny** (H.T.) F. Meilland, 1950. Peace × Signora. Indian yellow, outer petals shaded cerise. Blooms large and shapely in bud, opening rather loose, 30 petals. Very vigorous, 3–4 ft. Slight fragrance.

**Hector Deane** (H.T.) S. McGredy & Son, 1938. Salmon

pink, shaded gold. Medium-sized blooms, 25 petals. Vigorous, 2 ft. Delightfully fragrant.

**Hiawatha** (Wich. ramb.) M. H. Walsh, 1905. Crimson with white eye. Blooms produced in clusters, 5 petals. Very vigorous. Mid-July flowering. Prune A.

**Hinrich Gaede** (H.T.) W. Kordes, 1931. Nasturtium red shaded orange. Medium-sized blooms, urn shaped, 50 petals. Vigorous, 2 ft. Moderate fragrance.

**Hugh Dickson** (H.P.) Hugh Dickson, 1904. Crimson. Large full blooms, cupped, 36 petals. Very vigorous, 6 ft. and upwards. Very fragrant, Prune B.

**Innocence** (H.T.) Chaplin Bros., 1922. Pure white. Large semi-double blooms. Vigorous, 2–3 ft. Slight fragrance.

**Irene of Denmark** (Hy. poly.) Svend Poulsen, 1949. Mrs Cutbush × Edina. White, blooms small but compact, 2½ in. in diameter, 36 petals, in trusses, slight fragrance. Vigorous, 2 ft.

**Karl Herbst** (H.T.) Kordes, 1950. Independence × Peace. Scarlet. Blooms large and shapely, 50 petals. Vigorous, 2–3 ft. Very fragrant.

**Katherine Zeimet** (Polyantha) P. Lambert, 1901. Pure white. Small rosette blooms. A pretty, free-flowering variety. Light pruning will make compact bush, 2½ ft. Fragrant.

**Kirsten Poulsen** (Hy. poly.) Poulsen, 1925. Bright cherry red. Blooms large, 5 petals. Very vigorous, 3 ft. If lightly pruned will grow into a big bush. Susceptible to disease.

**Lady Belper** (H.T.) Verschuren, 1948. Light orange

shaded bronze. Blooms globular with high centre. Vigorous, sprawly growth, 2 ft. Fragrant.

**Lady Forteviot** (H.T.)  B. R. Cant & Sons, Ltd., 1928. Golden yellow, shaded apricot. Blooms large and loose, 20 petals. Vigorous, 2½ ft. Fragrant.

**Lady Gay** (Wich. ramb.)  M. H. Walsh, 1905. Rose pink. Rosette blooms, full, 35 petals. Very vigorous. July flowering. Prune A.

**Lady Godiva** (Wich. ramb.)  Paul & Son, 1908. Pale blush, deeper centre. Rosette blooms, full, 35 petals. Vigorous. Late July flowering. Almost evergreen foliage. Prune A.

**Lady Hillingdon** (Clg. T.)  Elisha J. Hicks, 1917. Apricot yellow, shaded fawn. Shapely medium-sized blooms, 24 petals. Vigorous. South or west wall. Prune B.

**Lady Sylvia**  Climbing Sport of dwarf variety. One of the best. Prune B.

**Lady Sylvia** (H.T.)  W. Stevens, 1927. Flesh pink, yellow base. Shapely medium-sized blooms, 32 petals. Vigorous, 2–3 ft. Fragrant. A sport from Mme Butterfly.

**Lavender Pinocchio** (Hy. poly.)  E. S. Boerner, Jackson & Perkins, 1948. Chocolate brown to pink bud opening to smoky lavender with yellow stamens, in clusters, individual blooms 2½ in. across. Moderately vigorous, 1½ to 2 ft. Fragrant.

**Lemon Pillar** (H.N.)  Paul & Son, 1915. Pale sulphur yellow. Blooms well shaped and full, 46 petals. Very vigorous. Summer flowering only. Prune B.

**Léontine Gervais** (Wich. ramb.)  Barbier, 1906. Salmon rose, tinted yellow. Blooms rosette and produced in large trusses. Vigorous. A fine variety. Mid-June flowering. Fragrant. Prune A.

**Lunelle** (H.T.)   Meilland, 1950. Peace × Columbia. Pink shaded gold. Blooms large and double, 50 petals. Vigorous and upright, 2 ft. Very fragrant.

**Maid of Honour** (Schleswig) (Hy. poly.)   W. Kordes, 1951. Holstein × Crimson Glory. Rich salmon pink suffused orange, lighter centre. Single blooms in trusses, individually 3½ in. across. Vigorous, 2–3 ft. Fragrant.

**Maréchal Niel** (N.)   Pradel, 1864. Deep bright golden yellow. Blooms full and globular, 60 petals. Vigorous climber. South or west wall. Prune B.

**Margot Anstiss** (H.T.)   A. Norman, 1947. Satin pink. Large shapely blooms, 45 petals. Free flowering. Vigorous, 2 ft. Tea fragrance.

**Mary Wallace** (Wich. ramb.)   Van Fleet, 1924. Clear bright rosy pink. Blooms very large and semi-double, 13 petals. Very vigorous. Late July flowering. North wall. Prune A.

**Mary Wheatcroft** (H.T.)   H. Robinson, 1943. Copper flame, dark-bronze foliage. Medium-sized loose bloom. Vigorous, 2½ ft. Fragrant.

**Masquerade** (Hy. poly.)   E. S. Boerner, Jackson & Perkins, 1950. Goldilocks × Holiday. Golden yellow buds opening to pink and changing gradually to deep red on the same large truss. Bushy, vigorous habit, 2 ft. Slight fragrance.

**McGredy's Ivory** (H.T.)   S. McGredy & Son, 1929. Creamy white shaded gold at base. Long pointed shapely blooms, 28 petals. Vigorous, 2 ft. 6 in. Fragrant.

**McGredy's Pink** (H.T.) S. McGredy & Son, 1936. Pale rose pink, shaded gold. Blooms large and shapely, 30 petals. Vigorous, 2 ft. Fragrant.

**McGredy's Sunset** (H.T.) S. McGredy & Son, 1937. Buttercup yellow, inside of petals flushed scarlet, shaded gold. Blooms cupped and loose, 25 petals. Moderately vigorous, 1½–2 ft. Fragrant.

**McGredy's Triumph** (H.T.) S. McGredy & Son, 1934. Fiery scarlet. Blooms large and loosely made, 26 petals. Vigorous, 2½ ft. Fragrant.

**McGredy's Yellow** (H.T.) S. McGredy & Son, 1933. Pale yellow. Blooms high pointed and shapely, 27 petals. Vigorous and branching, 2 ft. Fragrant. Susceptible to disease.

**Mermaid** (H. Brac.) W. Paul & Son, 1917. Pale sulphur yellow, with deep yellow stamens. Lovely, large single blooms. A very fine rose with handsome foliage. Prune B.

**Mev. G. A. Van Rossem** (H.T.) G. A. Van Rossem, 1926. Orange apricot on dark yellow ground. Medium-sized blooms, 25 petals. Vigorous, 2 ft. Fragrant.

**Michèle Meilland** (H.T.) Francis Meilland, 1948. Soft salmon rose pink. Long pointed blooms, 30 petals. Vigorous, 2 ft. Good for cutting. Slight fragrance.

**Minnehaha** (Wich. ramb.) Walsh, 1905. Deep pink. Small double blooms produced in large trusses. Very vigorous. Late summer flowering. Slight fragrance. Prune B.

**Mme Alfred Carrière** (H.N.) Schwartz, 1879. White, shaded blush. Blooms shapely. Vigorous climber. East or north wall. The best white climber. Blooms again in autumn. Very fragrant.

**Mme Butterfly** (H.T.)   The E. G. Hill Co., 1920. Pink, shaded apricot. Blooms shapely medium sized, 33 petals. Very vigorous, 3 ft. Sweetly fragrant. Very liable to attack by thrips.

**Mme Butterfly** (Clg. H.T.)   E. Percy-Smith, 1925. Pink, shaded apricot. South or west wall. Fragrant. Prune B. (Climbing counterpart of dwarf variety.)

**Mme Caroline Testout** (Clg. H. T.)   Chauvry, 1902. Climbing sport from Mme Caroline Testout. Reliable and free flowering. Prune B.

**Mme Edouard Herriot** (Clg. pern.)   Ketten, 1921. Terra-cotta passing to strawberry rose. Vigorous. Summer flowering only. Prune B.

**Mme Gregoire Staechelin** (Clg. H.T.)   Pedro Dot, 1927. Pale coral, pink shaded. Large semi-double blooms, 19 petals. Very vigorous. South or west wall. Very fragrant. Summer flowering only. Blooms from laterals. Prune B.

**Mme Henri Guillot** (H.T.)   Mallerin, 1938. Salmon pink, shaded orange. Cup-shaped blooms, 25 petals. Vigorous, 2 ft. Fragrant. The buds open rather flat.

**Mme Kriloff** (H.T.)   Meilland, 1949. Peace × Signora. Orange yellow, strongly veined carmine. Globular shaped blooms of good size, 35 petals. Vigorous and upright growth, $2\frac{1}{2}$ ft. Fragrant.

**Mme L. Dieudonné** (H.T.)   Meilland, 1950. Mme Joseph Perraud × J. B. Meilland. Vermilion, reverse gold. Blooms large, 4 in., double, 30 petals. Very vigorous, 2½ ft. Fragrant.

**Mme Yves Latieule** (H.T.) Meilland, 1949. Mme Joseph Perraud × Leonce Columbier. Primrose yellow. Blooms large and double, 70 petals. Vigorous, bushy habit, 2 ft. Moderate fragrance.

**Monique** (H.T.) Paolino, 1949. Lady Sylvia × unnamed seedling. Deep pink. Shapely globular blooms, 25 petals. Vigorous and upright, 2 ft. Very fragrant.

**Moonbeam** (H.T.) H. Robinson, 1950. Deep golden yellow. Large high centred bloom, 30 petals. Moderately vigorous, 1½ ft. Fragrant.

**Moonlight** (Hy. Musk) J. H. Pemberton, 1913. Lemon white. Blooms semi-double, 18 petals. Perpetual flowering. Very vigorous, 4–5 ft. Fragrant.

**Mrs Henry Bowles** (H.T.) Chaplin Bros., 1921. Glowing rose. Shapely large blooms, 30 petals. Vigorous. Fragrant.

**Mrs Henry Morse** (H.T.) S. McGredy & Son, 1919. Silvery rose pink. Large loose blooms, 27 petals. Vigorous, 2 ft. A very beautiful rose, but liable to disease.

**Mrs Herbert Stevens** (T.) S. McGredy & Son, 1910. White. Long pointed blooms, 25 petals. Vigorous and bushy, 2 ft. Fragrant.

**Mrs Sam McGredy** (H.T.) S. McGredy & Son, 1929. Coppery orange, flushed scarlet. Medium-sized blooms, 32 petals. Moderately vigorous, 1½ ft. Fragrant. Beautiful young foliage.

**Nevada** (Hy. Brac.) Pedro Dot, 1945. La Giralda × R. Moyesii. Cream flecked with crimson. Flowers large and single. Perpetual flowering. Large bush, 6 ft. shrub.

**Opera** (H.T.) Gaujard, 1949. La Belle Irisee × unnamed seedling. Light scarlet red with yellow base. Bud long pointed, flowers large, 30 petals. Vigorous, 2½ ft. Fragrant.

**Ophelia** (H.T.) W. Paul & Son, 1912. Salmon flesh. Medium-sized shapely blooms, 40 petals. Vigorous. Very fragrant. A very fine rose for cutting.

**Ophelia** (Clg. H.T.) A. Dickson & Sons, 1920. Very vigorous. South or west wall. Prune B.

**Orange Triumph** (Hy. poly.) W. Kordes, 1938. Orange red. Small full blooms, 36 petals. Vigorous, 3 ft. Quite free of disease. The blooms are produced in large clusters that remain over a long period. Very floriferous.

**Paul's Scarlet Climber** (Wich. climber) W. Paul & Son, 1916. Scarlet. Semi-double medium-sized blooms, 22 petals. Very vigorous. East wall. Remains in bloom over a long period.

**Pax** (Hy. Musk) J. H. Pemberton, 1918. Trier × Sunburst. White. Blooms 3–4 in., 18 petals. Vigorous, 4–5 ft. Very free flowering. Fragrant.

**Peace** (H.T.) Francis Meilland, 1947. Light yellow shades, the petals edged rose pink. Large, full, long-lasting blooms. Vigorous. Delicate fragrance.

**Penelope** (Hy. Musk) J. H. Pemberton, 1923. Shell pink, shaded salmon. Medium semi-double blooms, 24 petals. Very vigorous, 5 ft. Fragrant. Perpetual flowering.

**Percy Izzard** (H.T.) H. Robinson, 1936. Cream, shaded yellow. Large shapely blooms, 22 petals. Moderately vigorous, 1½ to 2 ft. Fragrant.

84

**Perle d'Or** (Hy. poly). Dubreuil, 1883. Nankeen yellow. Very miniature blooms, perfectly formed. One of the best of its class. Requires little pruning. Height, 15 in. to 3 ft.

**Phyllis Bide** (Hy. wich.) S. Bide & Sons, 1923. Carmine pink, shaded yellow. Small blooms, 24 petals. Vigorous, 6 ft. Fragrant. Very perpetual. Prune B.

**Phyllis Gold** (H.T.) H. Robinson, 1934. Golden yellow. Large shapely blooms, 26 petals. Vigorous, 2½ ft. Fragrant. Susceptible to disease.

**Picture** (H.T.) S. McGredy & Son, 1932. Clear rose pink. Cup-shaped blooms, 24 petals. Moderately vigorous, 2 ft. Slight fragrance. Not liable to disease. A very lovely rose.

**Pilar Landecho** (H.T.) Nadal, 1939. Coppery orange, shaded pink. Long pointed blooms, 36 petals. Very vigorous, 2½ ft. Fragrant.

**Pinocchio** (Rosenmarchen) (Hy. poly.) W. Kordes, 1949. Eva × Geheimrat Duisberg. Warm pink small rosette double flowers in large trusses. Vigorous, 2 ft.

**Poinsettia** (H.T.) Howard & Smith. Mrs J. D. Eisele × Vaterland × J. C. Thornton. Bright unfading scarlet. Bud long pointed, medium size, 28 petals. Vigorous and compact, 2 ft. Slight fragrance.

**Polly** (H.T.) G. Beckwith & Son, 1928. Cream shaded pink and gold. Blooms shapely and of medium size, 35 petals. Vigorous, 2 ft. Fragrant. Very floriferous and good for cutting.

**Poulsen's Pink** (Hy. poly.) Poulsen, 1939. Pink, shaded

gold. Semi-double, cupped and produced in clusters, 12 petals. Vigorous, 1½–2 ft. Fragrant.

**Poulsen's Supreme** (Hy. poly.) Svend Poulsen, 1949. Rose pink. Small flowers, 2 in., 8 petals, slight fragrance. Growth upright and free, 2 ft.

**Poulsen's Yellow** (Hy. poly.) Poulsen, 1938. Buttercup yellow. The semi-double blooms are produced in clusters throughout the season, 17 petals. Moderately vigorous, 1½ ft.

**President Charles Hain** (H.T.) L. Reymond, 1929. Pale yellow, shaded cream. Blooms large and shapely, 54 petals. Vigorous, 2½ ft. Fragrant. An enormous rose. Intolerant of damp.

**President Hoover** (H.T.) Coddington, 1930. Glowing orange yellow, shaded pink. Blooms fairly large and freely produced, 24 petals. Vigorous, a rather lanky grower, 2–3 ft. Fragrant.

**Prosperity** (Hy. moschata) Pemberton, 1919. Marie-Jeanne × Perle des Jeannes. White. Large clusters of rosette-shaped blooms. Vigorous, 6–8 ft. Musk fragrance.

**Purity** (Wich. ramb.) Hoopes & Thomas, 1917. Pure white. Large semi-double blooms, 15 petals. Very vigorous. Handsome foliage. Very fragrant. Late June flowering. Will sometimes bloom again in the autumn. Prune B.

**Red Ensign** (H.T.) A. Norman, 1947. Southport × Crimson Glory. Deep crimson. A very large well-formed exhibition and garden rose. Vigorous, 2½ ft. Strong damask fragrance. Blooms inclined to ball.

**Rex Anderson** (H.T.) S. McGredy & Son, 1937. Cream,

shaded gold at base of petals. Large shapely blooms, 38 petals. Very vigorous, 2½ ft. Fragrant.

**Rosa × alba** White. Blooms flat, almost double, produced in small clusters. June flowering. Vigorous, 8 ft. Fragrant.

**Rosa × alba Celestial** Warm pink, 6 ft. June flowering.

**Rosa × alba Maiden's Blush** Large warm pink, full flowers, 6–8 ft.

**Rosa × alba maxima** Creamy white, large and double, 6–8 ft. Very fragrant.

**Rosa bracteata** The Macartney Rose, China. Creamy white single blooms 3 in. across. Very good climber for sheltered position. Prune B.

**Rosa Ecae** (E.C. Aitchinson) Buttercup yellow. Blooms small and freely produced. Decorative fernlike foliage. Vigorous shrub, 6 ft. Prune B.

**Rosa Harrisonii** (Austrian Brier) Soft golden yellow. Blooms small and semi-double. Vigorous shrub, 6–8 ft.

**Rosa Hugonis** 'The Golden Rose of China'. Single early blooms produced freely in early June. Vigorous shrub, 6–8 ft.

**Rosa moschata** (Musk Rose) White blooms, 1½–2 in. diameter produced in large trusses, June and July. Very vigorous climber. Prune B.

**Rosa Moyesii** Blood red. Blooms medium size. Bottle-shaped autumn fruits. Vigorous, 10 ft.

**Rosa Moyesii Nevada** Pale flesh. Blooms semi-double, 3½ in. Graceful shrub up to 7 ft. Continuous flowering.

**Rosa rugosa Schneezwerg** Pure white. Scarlet heps after

the first flush of flowering appear concurrently with the later flush of bloom. Shrub up to 6 ft.

**Rosa sericea pteracantha** White. Shrub noteworthy for its translucent and huge red thorns on the young wood. Shrub, 8–10 ft.

**Rosa spinosissima** 'The Scots Briers' or Burnet Roses. Prickly dense bushes up to 6 ft. in height in various colours. Do best in poor, sandy soils.

**Rose Berkley** (H.T.) S. McGredy & Son, 1928. Salmon pink, suffused orange. Blooms large and shapely, 52 petals. Vigorous, 2 ft. Fragrant.

**Rubáiyát** (H.T.) S. McGredy & Son, 1949. Rose cerise with lighter shades on the outer petals. Flowers large and well formed, 25 petals. Very vigorous, 3 ft. Very fragrant.

**Salmon Perfection** (Hy. poly.) De Ruiter, 1950. Dark salmon with orange shading. Small flowers, of 25 petals, in very large trusses. Vigorous, 2 ft. Slight fragrance.

**Sam McGredy** (H.T.) S. McGredy & Son, 1937. Buff, shaded cream. Extremely large blooms, 18 petals. Moderately vigorous, 1½ ft. An exhibitor's rose.

**Sanders' White** (Wich. ramb.) Sanders, 1915. Pure white. Small rosette-shaped blooms produced in large clusters, 35 petals. Late June flowering. Fragrant. Prune A.

**Shot Silk** (H.T.) A. Dickson & Sons, 1924. Cerise shaded orange salmon. Lovely in bud, cup-shaped blooms, 27 petals. Moderately vigorous, 1½ ft. Very fragrant. A beautiful bedding rose which should be planted closely.

**Shot Silk** (Clg. H.T.) Prince, 1937. Cerise, shaded

orange salmon. Vigorous. A climbing sport from the dwarf variety. Prune B.

**Show Girl** (H.T.) Lammerts, Armstrong Nurseries, 1949. Joanna Hill × Crimson Glory. Deep pink. Large, well-shaped blooms freely produced, 22 petals. Vigorous, $2\frac{1}{2}$ ft. Fragrant.

**Signora** (H.T.) D. Aicardi, 1936. Julien Potin × Sensation. Orange and flame red. Well-shaped, cupped blooms, 27 petals. Vigorous, 2–$2\frac{1}{2}$ ft. Fragrant.

**Sir Henry Segrave** (H.T.) A. Dickson & Sons, 1932. Primrose yellow. Large and shapely blooms, 45 petals. Moderately vigorous, $1\frac{1}{2}$ ft. Blooms rather impatient of wet. Fragrant.

**Souvenir Jacques Verschuren** (H.T.) J. Verschuren Pechtold, 1950. Katherine Pechtold × Orange Delight. Bicolour red and salmon. Moderately large full blooms, 32 petals. Vigorous, 2 ft. Fragrant.

**Spek's Yellow** (H.T.) H. A. Verschuren, 1947. Deep brilliant yellow. Small shapely blooms, 35 petals. Vigorous tall growth, $2\frac{1}{2}$ ft. Fragrant. A variety which keeps its colour well.

**Stanwell Perpetual** (Perpetual Scotch) Lee. Pale blush. Medium-sized double blooms. Vigorous, 6 ft. Flowers very early and is also good in autumn. Very fragrant. Prune B.

**Sutter's Gold** (H.T.) Swim, Armstrong Nurseries, 1950. Charlotte Armstrong × Signora. Orange yellow overlaid Indian red. Blooms large with high pointed centre, 24 petals. Vigorous upright growth, $2\frac{1}{2}$ ft. Strong fragrance.

**Suzon Lotthé** (H.T.) Meilland, 1949. Peace × Signora.

White to apple pink, petals edged cerise. Globular blooms with high pointed centre, 40 petals. Vigorous, 2 ft. Fragrant.

**Talisman** (H.T.) Montgomery Co., 1929. Scarlet, pink, copper and gold shadings. Urn-shaped blooms, 30 petals. Moderately vigorous, 1½ ft. Fragrant.

**Texas Centennial** (H.T.) Watkins, 1935. President Hoover sport. Vermilion red, gold at base. Blooms shapely and long, 25 petals. Vigorous, 2 ft. Fragrant.

**The Doctor** (H.T.) Howard & Smith, 1939. Bright silvery rose. Large blooms, shapely in bud, opening rather loose, 29 petals. Moderately vigorous, 1½ ft. Delightfully fragrant. Opens to an enormous bloom that lasts over a long period.

**Thelma** (Wich. ramb.) W. Easlea & Sons, 1927. Delicate coral pink. Semi-double blooms, 3 in. when open, produced in small clusters, 17 petals. Early July flowering. Prune A.

**The New Dawn** (Wich. ramb.) Dreer, 1930. Soft delicate pink. Blooms cupped of medium size, 34 petals. Moderately vigorous, 6–10 ft. A moderately growing sport from Dr Van Fleet. Perpetual flowering. Early July onwards. Prune B.

**Vanity** (Hy. moschata) Pemberton, 1920. Rose pink. Semi-double blooms produced in large sprays. Very vigorous, 8 ft. Musk fragrance.

**Van Nes** (Hy. poly.) Leenders, 1934. Cochineal carmine. The semi-double blooms are rather large, with peculiar frilled edges. Also known by the American name Permanent Wave. Vigorous, 2–3 ft. Slight fragrance.

**Violinista Costa** (H.T.)   Camprubi Nadal, 1937. Scarlet, shaded strawberry gold. Loose globular blooms, 44 petals. Vigorous and sprawling, 1½–2 ft. Fragrant. A very fine variety that is disease resistant. Lovely in the autumn.

**Virgo** (H.T.)   Charles Mallerin, 1947. Pole Nord × Neige Parfum. White. High-pointed, medium-sized blooms of good shape, 25 petals. Vigorous and bushy, 2 ft. Slight fragrance.

**Vogue** (Hy. poly.)   E. S. Boerner, Jackson & Perkins, 1949. Pinocchio (Rosenmarchen) × Crimson Glory. Colour rose dove pink, 2½ in., 23 petals. Vigorous, 2–2½ ft. Fragrant.

**W. E. Chaplin** (H.T.)   Chaplin Bros., Ltd., 1931. Deep crimson. Large, high centred blooms, 26 petals. Vigorous, 2 ft. Blooms hold their colour well.

**William Harvey** (H.T.)   A. Norman, 1946. Southport × Crimson Glory. Deep scarlet crimson. Very large blooms of excellent shape, 28 petals. Vigorous and upright, 2½ ft. Very fragrant.

**William Moore** (H.T.)   S. McGredy & Son, 1935. Deep pink, becoming lighter as the flowers expand. Large, cupped blooms, 33 petals. Vigorous, 2 ft. Fragrant.

**William Orr** (H.T.)   S. McGredy & Son, 1931. Deep velvety crimson. Buds long pointed, blooms large and high centred, 45 petals. Fragrant. Moderately vigorous, 1¼ ft. Very fragrant.

**Yellow Pinocchio** (Hy. poly.)   E. S. Boerner, Jackson & Perkins, 1950. Goldilocks × Marionette. Yellow, turning paler and with pink edging. Individual blooms of 35 petals opening to 2½ in., in clusters. Growth moderate and bushy, 2 ft. Moderate fragrance.

**Yvonne Rabier** (Hy. poly.)   Turbat & Co., 1910. White. Rosette-shaped blooms very freely produced, 36 petals. Very free and perpetual flowering. Vigorous, 2–3 ft. Fragrant.

**Zephirine Drouhin** (H.B.)   Bizot, 1873. Bright carmine pink. Blooms large, 20 petals. Very vigorous, 10 ft. South or west wall. Thornless. Very fragrant. Prune B.